BASIC COMMUNICATION SKILLS OF ENGLISH

NON-VERBAL SKILLS, LISTENING SKILLS, READING SKILLS, WRITING SKILLS, E – SKILLS, INTERVIEW SKILLS.

DR ANSHUMALI PANDEY

Contents

Foreword   *v*

Preface   *vii*

1. Communication   1

2. Non-verbal Communication   20

3. Listening Skills   33

4. Reading Skills   44

5. Writing Skills   59

6. Proposals   87

7. Reports Writing   101

8. Letter Writing   109

9. E-skills   123

10. Interview Skills   149

The Author   157

Foreword

Your ability to communicate clearly and share thoughts, feelings and ideas will help you in all your relations with other people. As a student, you may study any language, but it is important that you are able to read, write, speak and listen well in order to communicate properly. Speaking more than one language can help you to communicate well with people around the world. Learning English can help you to communicate with people who understand English besides the language you have been exposed to in your family, for example, your mother tongue.

*Back in the early days of pre-globalization, knowing English was a plus. Like it or not, it was a mark of superior knowledge and sophistication. It made you look impressive to people. Now, regardless of your background and upbringing, many bosses will automatically expect you to know the language. Even if you received education in a different language or come from a place where English is barely spoken. Today you are expected to know English. This means that in order to impress your interviewer or boss now, **you have to show that you are extremely fluent and competent in both speaking and writing the language**.*

This book will certainly be of help to you.

Preface

Communication is the act of transferring information from one place, person or group to another. The transmission of the message from sender to recipient can be affected by variety of factors. These include our emotions, cultural situation, medium used to communicate, and even our location. The complexity is why good communication skills are considered so desirable by employers around the world while accurate, effective, and unambiguous communication is actually extremely hard.

Communication can have several different forms such as verbal or spoken, non-verbal, written, and visualization. This includes telephonic conversation, written communication such as letter and e-mail conversations. The term requires an element of success in transmitting or imparting a message, whether information, ideas, or emotions.

For our communication to be impactful, we need to learn about the essential parts of verbal, non-verbal, and written communication skills as well as the process, levels and flow of communication. Several barriers to effective communication must be kept in mind to make our communication a success.

Happy Reading and Best wishes,

Dr. Anshumali Pandey

COMMUNICATION

INTRODUCTION:

Communication is the act of transferring information from one place, person or group to another. The transmission of the message from sender to recipient can be affected by variety of factors. These include our emotions, cultural situation, medium used to communicate, and even our location. The complexity is why good communication skills are considered so desirable by employers around the world while accurate, effective, and unambiguous communication is actually extremely hard.

Communication can have several different forms such as verbal or spoken, non-verbal, written, and visualization. This includes telephonic conversation, written communication such as letter and e-mail conversations. The term requires an element of success in transmitting or imparting a message, whether information, ideas, or emotions.

For our communication to be impactful, we need to learn about the essential parts of verbal, non-verbal, and written communication skills as well as the process, levels and flow of communication. Several barriers to effective communication must be kept in mind to make our communication a success.

<u>OBJECTIVES</u>

After the successful completion of this chapter, you will be able to-

- Understand, explain and define communication.
- Describe the different types of communication.
- Understand the process and levels of communication.
- Understand the flow of communication.
- Understand the barriers to effective communication.

WHAT IS COMMUNICATION?

Communication plays a vital role in our daily life. For all fields of endeavour we need good communication skill. Whatever profession you have, whether you are an engineer, doctor or an employee of any organization, having a firm grasp of communication will undoubtedly play a key role in your success. So, we must first understand what communication is and what different types of communication are.

Communication is the act of transferring information from one place, person or group to another. Every communication involves (at least) one sender, a message and a recipient. This may sound simple, but communication is actually a very complex subject. The transmission of the message from sender to recipient can be affected by variety of things. These include our emotions, the cultural situation, the medium used to communicate, and even our location. The complexity is why good communication skills are considered so desirable by employers around the world.

Accurate, effective and unambiguous communication is actually extremely hard. In other words, communication is more than simply the transmission of information. The term requires an element of success in transmitting or imparting a message, whether information, ideas, or emotions.

Often at times, people with great technical skills reach a point in their careers where they are no longer promoted, because of their inability to communicate effectively. Professors often tell anecdotal stories about students that have been hugely successful in gaining jobs right out of college, but then struggle to get promoted into management and leadership roles beyond their technical duties. This is because they lack in one fundamental skill that would have helped them shine above all their competition is 'communication'.

CATEGORIES OF COMMUNICATION

There are wide ranges of ways in which we communicate, and more than one may occur at any given time. The different categories of communication include:

- Spoken or Verbal Communication
- Non-Verbal communication
- Written Communication
- Visual Communication

Spoken or Verbal Communication-

Verbal communication is the use of language to transfer information through speaking or sign language. This includes face-to-face, telephone, radio or television, and other media. It is one of the most common types, often used during presentations, video conferences, phone calls, meetings, and one-on-one conversations. Verbal communication is important because it is efficient. It can help support verbal communication with both nonverbal and written communication.

Non-Verbal Communication-

Non-verbal communication is the use of body language, gestures, and facial expressions to convey information to others. It can be used both intentionally and unintentionally. For example, you might smile unintentionally when you hear a pleasing or enjoyable idea or a piece of information. Non-verbal communication is helpful when trying to understand others thoughts and feelings. There are many subtle ways that we communicate (perhaps even unintentionally) with others. For example, the tone of voice can give clues to mood or emotional state, while hand signals or gestures can add to a spoken message.

If someone displays "closed" body language such as crossed arms or legs, or hunched shoulders, he/she might be feeling anxious, angry, or nervous. If they display "open" body language with both feet on the floor and arms by their side or on the table, they are likely feeling positive and open to information.

Written Communication-

Written communication is the act of writing, typing or printing symbols like letters and numbers to convey information. It is helpful because it provides a record of information for reference. Writing is commonly used to share information through books, pamphlets, blogs, letters, memos, and more. Emails and chats are a common form of written communication in the workplace.

This includes letters, e-mails, social media, books, magazines, internet, and other media. Until recent times, relatively small number of writers and publishers were very powerful when it came to communicating the written word. Today, we can all write and publish our ideas online, which have led to an explosion of information and communication possibilities.

Visual Communication-

Visual communication is the act of using photographs, art, drawings, sketches, charts, and graphs to convey information. Visuals are often used as an aid during presentations to provide helpful context alongside written and/or verbal communication. People have different learning styles; visual communication might be more helpful for some to consume ideas and information.

Graphs and charts, maps, logos, and other visualizations can all communicate messages. The process of interpersonal communication cannot be regarded as a phenomena which simply 'happen'. Instead, it must be seen as a process that involves participants who negotiate their roles with each other, whether consciously or unconsciously. The sender sends a message or communication through a communication channel to one or more recipients.

IMPROVING COMMUNICATION SKILL

Here are a few steps that you can take to develop your verbal communication skills:

- **Use a strong, confident speaking voice-** Especially when presenting information to a few or a group of people, be sure to use a strong voice so that everyone can easily hear you. Be confident when speaking so that your ideas are clear and easy for others to understand.
- **Use active listening-** The other side of using verbal communication is intently listening and hearing others. Active listening skills are key when conducting a meeting, presentation or even when participating in a one-on-one conversation, doing so will help you grow as a communicator.
- **Avoid filler words-** It can be tempting, especially during a presentation, to use filler words such as "um," "like," "so" or "yeah." While it might feel natural after completing a sentence or pausing to collect your thoughts, it can also be distracting for your audience. Try presenting to a trusted friend or colleague who can call attention to the times you use filler words. Try to replace them by taking a breath when you are tempted to use them.

NOTE- Few steps that you can take to develop your Non-verbal communication skills are-

- **Notice how your emotions feel physically-** Throughout the day, as you experience a range of emotions (anything from energized, bored, happy or frustrated), try to identify where you feel that emotion within your body. Developing self-awareness around how your emotions affect your body can give you greater mastery over your external presentation.

- **Be intentional about your nonverbal communications-** Make an effort to display positive body language when you feel alert, open, and positive about your surroundings. You can also use body language to support your verbal communication if you feel confused or anxious about information, like using a furrowed brow. Use body language alongside verbal communication, such as asking to follow up questions or pulling the presenter aside to give feedback.

- **Mimic nonverbal communications, you find effective-** If you find certain facial expressions or body language beneficial to a certain setting, use it as a guide when improving your own nonverbal communications. For example, if you see that when someone nods their head, it communicates approval and positive feedback efficiently, use it in your next meeting when you have the same feelings.

NOTE- Few steps that you can take to develop your written communication skills are-

- **Strive for simplicity-** Written communications should be as simple and clear as possible. While it might be helpful to include lots of detail in instructional communications, for example, you should look for areas where you can write as clearly as possible for your audience to understand.

- **Do not rely on tone-**Always be careful when you are trying to communicate a certain tone when writing because you do not have the nuance of verbal and nonverbal communications, for example, attempting to communicate a joke, sarcasm, or excitement might be translated differently depending on the audience. Instead, try to keep your writing as simple and plain as possible and follow up with verbal communications where you can add more personality.

- **Take time to review your written communications-** Setting time aside to re-read your emails, letters, or memos can help you identify mistakes or opportunities to say something differently. For important communications or those that will be sent to a large number of people, it might be helpful to have a trusted colleague review it as well.
- **Keep a file of writing you find productive or enjoyable-** If you receive a certain pamphlet, email or memo that you find particularly helpful or interesting, save it for reference when writing your own communications. Incorporating methods or styles you like can help you to improve over time.

NOTE- Few steps that you can take to develop your visual communication skills are-

- Ask others before including visuals. If you are considering sharing a visual aid in your presentation or email, consider asking others for feedback. Adding visuals can sometimes make concepts confusing or muddled. Getting a third-party perspective can help you decide whether the visual adds value to your communications.
- Consider your audience. Be sure to include visuals that are easily understood by your audience. For example, if you are displaying a chart with unfamiliar data, be sure to take time and explain what is happening in the visual and how it relates to what you are saying. You should never use sensitive, offensive, violent or graphic visuals in any form.

To make improvements to your communication skills, set personal goals to work through the things you want to accomplish step by step. It might be helpful to consult with trusted colleagues, managers or mentors to identify which areas would be best to focus on first.

NEED FOR EFFECTIVE COMMUNICATION

Besides the workplace and personal relationships, here are some other reasons why good communication is important-

Understanding-

For better understanding what you want, what your need is and what is your intention, it is desirable to have to communicate well. It can be

the determining factor in negotiating a salary or setting the course of a friendship or relationship. Often conflicts, arguments, and disagreements stem from not communicating clearly. Preventing these misunderstandings is one reason, communication is crucial.

Strengthening Relationships-

This is because building a rapport with someone comes from talking and listening. When you can get to know each other and discover similarities, your relationship can build a more solid foundation. This applies to anything in life: clients, friendships, and more.

Relieving Stress-

Whenever you are feeling overwhelmed, it is a great relief to get things off your chest by discussing your problems with friends. This discussion also helps you to see your problems from new perspectives.

Increasing Confidence-

Communicating clearly means that people will be more apt to listen to you. Not only will you sound more intelligent, but will more easily get your point across. And when people value what you say, your self-esteem naturally increases.

Happiness-

With the better upward mobility in the workplace, stronger relationships, lower stress, and increased self-esteem, you should find yourself happier all around.

Communicating effectively is a powerful tool, and improving your skill set will lead you to a drastically more fulfilling life, both personally and professionally. Set yourself now on the path to increased happiness and prosperity by vowing to work on your communication skills every day.

Hence, we can say communication has three parts:

1. **The sender,**
2. **The message**
3. **The recipient.**

The sender 'encodes' the message, usually in a mixture of words and non-verbal communication. It is transmitted in some way (for example, in speech or writing), and the recipient 'decodes' it. The sender must encode the message (the information being conveyed) into a form that is appropriate to the communication channel, and the recipient then decodes the message to understand its meaning and significance.

Of course, there may be more than one recipient, and the complexity of communication means that each one may receive a slightly different message. Two people may read very different things into the choice of words and/or body language. It is also possible that neither of them will have quite the same understanding as to the sender.

In face-to-face communication, the roles of the sender and recipient are not distinct. The two roles will pass back and forwards between two people talking. Both parties communicate with each other, even if in very subtle ways such as through eye-contact (or lack of) and general body language. In written communication, however, the sender and recipient are more distinct.

THE PROCESS OF COMMUNICATION

Communication is a process of the exchange of information between the sender and the receiver. It always processes around us because we communicate to live as well as understand with each other in order to express what we are thinking. But, sometime a communication may fail to present, or sometimes the receiver misunderstands what the sender is trying to give the information. Therefore, some skills help us have better and effective communication. According to researchers, there are five steps of the communication process: sender has an idea, sender decodes the idea in a message, message travels over channel, receiver decodes the message and lastly feedback travel back to the sender.

The process of communication refers to the transmission or passage of information or message from the sender through a selected channel to the receiver overcoming barriers that affect its pace. The process of communication is a cyclic as it begins with the sender and ends with the sender in the form of feedback.

The essential elements of the process of communication are the message, the sender, encoding, the channel, the receiver, decoding, acting on the message, the feedback, and the communication environment. Both the sender and the receiver play a role in making communication effective.

The five steps of the Communication Process:

The steps on the theory of five steps communication process are encoding, planning, medium, decoding, and lastly the feedback. There is the key point of explaining this assignment and the correct way to ensure the intended audient received the right message. On the page below will have the 5 steps of the communication process-

1. Encoding

Encoding process involves translating an idea. Therefore, the idea will need to be changed into ordinary language with letter or symbols to pass on the information to the other party. However, the information of encoding is not yet sending out the message to the channel, messages are only an idea that thinking in the sender. Besides, the sender might not have plan of which the sending ways are the better way for the receiver. So, encoding is just an idea that came out from the sender mind, and when the sender starts to plan for sending out the message, it is the second step of the communication process, i.e. planning.

2. Planning

The second step of the communication process includes the processes of organization and sending. After encoding an idea, the sender will start to plan how to send the message. For example, the sender uses a letter to send the message, he or she will translate the idea to an ordinary language or symbols into words, the sender will make sure to use simple comprehendible words for the receiver. Therefore, the receiver will easily get the correct message from the sender rather than having communication gaps of misrepresentation and misunderstanding. To cater it when the sender organizes the message, he/she make sure to double confirm on the grammar and sentence meaning. When it is confirmed to be a right message, it will come to choose the types of how the sender will use to send out the message to the receiver.

3. Medium

The information that the sender wants to communicate is transmitted over a channel through which the message travels to the receiver. A channel or a medium connects the sender to the receiver. Medium of communication may include a memorandum, a computer, a telephone, a telegram, or a television. The choice of a channel depends on the communication situation. For instance, when dealing with confidential information, direct face-to-face interaction or a sealed letter are more effective mediums than a telephone conversation.

4. Decoding

The receiver is the person to whom the message is transmitted. In order to decode the message, the receiver has to be ready to receive the message. That is the receiver should not be preoccupied with other thoughts that might cause him to pay insufficient attention to the message. Decoding refers to the process of translation of symbols encoded by the sender into ideas that can be understood. Communication can be considered effective only when both the sender and the receiver attach similar meanings to the symbol that compose the message. Communication is not complete unless it is understood by both the sender and the receiver.

5. Feedback

A message generated by the receiver in response to the sender's original message is known as feedback. Feedback is necessary to ensure that the message has been effectively encoded, transmitted, decoded and understood. It helps a sender evaluate the effectiveness of his message, so that he can modify his subsequent messages. Feedback also confirms whether there has been any change in the behaviour of the individual or in the organization as a result of communication.

Some other communication processes are-

Besides, the five types of the communication process, there are some other types of communication processes to ensure that the intended audience receives the right message.

Body Language

Body language is the unspoken element, of communication that we use to reveal our true feelings and emotions. Our gestures, facial expressions and postures. For instance, when we are able to read these signs, we can use it to our advantage. For example, it can help us to understand the complete message of what someone is trying to say to us, and to enhance our awareness of people's reactions to what we say and do.

We can also use it to adjust our own body language so that we appear more positive, engaging and approachable.

Noise

Noise is anything that has a disturbing influence on the message. Since noise hinders communication, the sender should choose a channel that is free from noise. Noise may occur at the sender's end, during transmission, or at the receiver's end.

Levels of communication:

Communication between two people occurs on numerous levels simultaneously, each with its nuances and complexities. These levels of communication are verbal, physical, auditory, emotional, and energetic.

1. Verbal Level of Communication

This is perhaps the most apparent level of human communication. People can spend a lifetime trying to master it. This level includes our selection of words based on an understanding between the speaker and the listener. There are multiple definitions for most words and few of hold the same meaning for each word. Different words evoke different images, memories, and meaning for different people.

To communicate effectively on the verbal level, select the "right" words and understand the context of the conversation (including moral, religious, ethnic and religious differences). Be clear and concise. When possible, formulate your thoughts to avoid rambling. This is an art in itself.

2. Physical Level of Communication

Communication with eye contact, gestures, movements, stances, breathing, posture, and facial expressions influence how we communicate. When used with integrity, techniques like "matching and mirroring" people's posture and gestures, including certain words too can increase the receptivity of your message.

To communicate effectively on the physical level, it is helpful to physically align with others, connecting with them in form and movement.

It also helps to be mindful of your posture, facial expressions, and hand gestures.

3. Auditory Level of Communication

The sound of our voice, including the tone, range, volume, and speed affects how our messages are received and interpreted by others. For example, fast talkers will find it beneficial to slow their speech when speaking to a thoughtful, introverted person.

Also, how we enunciate, inflect, and emphasize on certain words affects how others interpret the meaning of what we say. To communicate effectively on the auditory level, become aware of various auditory cues, speaking to others in a manner more akin to their ways (another form of "matching and mirroring").

4. Emotional Level of Communication

Few people appreciate how our emotional state affects what we communicate and how the recipient interprets the message. Are you more receptive to someone who is positive and life- affirming or one who is negative and critical, enthusiastic or dull?

The speaker's emotions put the recipient in a particular state of mind and influence how the listener interprets what is said. To communicate effectively on the emotional level become aware of your emotional state, learning to pause and release negative emotions before attempting to connect with others. Words delivered with pride, anger or fears are rarely well- received.

5. Energetic Level of Communication

This is also called the psychic level. This level of communication encompasses a vast range of unseen factors including, an individual's level of consciousness, frequency or harmonics of the message, and other subtle energies.

Some people seem to have an "X-factor"—a unique presence—that naturally imparts their messages to others with greater receptivity and understanding.

To communicate more effectively, hold the highest intention for the other person's wellbeing. This requires a unique level of mindfulness generally cultivated through compassion practices. When we are centred in a state of mastery, we are more likely to access this psychic dimension that holds great treasures of insights into others, helping us communicate with greater ease.

6. **Bringing all the levels of communication together**

The verbal level is the content; it is what we say. The physical, auditory, emotional, and energetic levels represent how we convey a message. These levels of communication are interdependent, as each level affects the other.

For example, our emotional state affects our body language, and our feelings influence our emotional state. Simply becoming aware of these various levels can be beneficial.

When we see complexities inherent in human communication, we can be made more patient in our speech and more compassionate towards others and ourselves.

FLOW OF COMMUNICATION

Communication is vital to organizational life. Organizations exist through communication without communication, there would be no organizations. As Herbert Simon expresses it, "Without communication, there can be no organizations, for there is no possibility then of the group influencing the behavior of the individual."

Therefore, communication is the ingredient that makes organizations possible. It is the vehicle through which the basic managerial functions are carried out. Managers direct organizational activities through communication. They coordinate through communication, and they plan, organize, motivate, and control through communication. Virtually all actions taken in an organization has been preceded by communication. Thus, communication is an essential ingredient of almost everything a manager does.

In an organization where we work, there are major communication systems. Communication flow downward, upward or horizontally. As these terms are used frequently in organizations, we need some clarification of each, which are as follows:

Downward Communication-

Downward communication is from superior to subordinate, i.e. from boss to employees and from managers to operating staff. In any work place, managers communicate with their

employees for job instruction which includes teaching new or current employees how to do a particular task. They pass upon a organizational goal and train employee to achieve those goals. Managers also do communicate with their employees to give them a feedback upon their performance. They also take a role in having appraisal or superior's evaluation of employee performance. Downward communication flow is of course, related to the hierarchical structure of the organization. Messages seem to get larger as they travel downward through successive levels of the organization. A simple instruction given at the top of the hierarchy, for example, may become a formal plan for operation at a lower level.

Upward Communication-

Upward communication is equally important for effective communication. Upward communication travels from lower to higher ranks in the hierarchy. Various mechanisms are used by organizations to facilitate upward communication. Suggestion boxes, group meetings, grievance procedures, participate decision-making are some examples. This is maintained to get feedback to managers from employees.

In general, in any organization employees talk to superiors about themselves, their fellow employees, job satisfaction, perceptions of their work, feelings and opinions about organizational goals and policies. The feedback that the management receives from the lower level is thus extremely important and it should be encouraged. However, one must remember if the right climate is not created employees may not provide their feedback freely and accurately.

Diagonal Communication-

Diagonal communication is cross-functional communication between employees at different levels of the organization. For example, if the vice president of sales sends an e-mail to the vice president of manufacturing asking when a product will be available for shipping, this is an example of horizontal communication. However, if a sales representative e-mails the vice president of marketing, then diagonal communication has occurred. Whenever communication goes from one department to another department, the sender's manager should be made part of the loop. A manager may be put in an embarrassing position and appear incompetent if he is not aware of everything happening in his department. Trust may be lost and careers damaged by not paying attention to key communication protocols.

Diagonal communication is becoming more common in organizations with a flattened, matrix, or product-based structure. The advantages of such communication include:

- Building relationships between senior-level and lower-level employees from different parts of the organization.
- Encouraging an informal flow of information in the organization.
- Reducing the chance of a message being distorted by going through additional filters.
- Reducing the workloads of senior-level managers.

Horizontal or Lateral Communication-
Much information needs to be shared among people on the same hierarchical level. Such horizontal or lateral communication takes place among people in the same work team (see fig 1.2). Hence, this form of communication is beneficial for achieving coordination. Different units coordinate activities by such communication are required to accomplish task goals. Inter-departmental uniformity may be achieved through diagonal communication. Such communication takes place through telephone calls, short memos and notes, face-to-face interactions, etc.

Although this type of communication is not often encouraged, it is sure to take place. Workers at the same level tend to talk with one another about their work, supervisors, and working conditions. They also talk with one another about various personal and non-work problems. As a result, horizontal communication can contribute to self-maintenance goals as well as to task goals. Horizontal or lateral communication takes place through informal channels.

BARRIERS TO EFFECTIVE COMMUNICATION

The process of communication has multiple barriers. The intended communication will often be disturbed and distorted leading to a condition of misunderstanding and failure of communication. The barriers to effective communication could be of many types like linguistic, psychological, emotional, physical, cultural, etc. Below, we will discuss these types in detail-

Linguistic Barriers-

The language barrier is one of the main barriers that limit effective communication. Language is the most commonly employed tool of communication. The fact that each major region has its own language is another barrier to effective communication. Sometimes even a thick dialect may render the communication ineffective.

As per some estimates, the dialects of every two regions changes within a few kilometers. Even in the same workplace, different employees will have different linguistic skills. As a result, the communication channels that span across the organization would be affected by this. Thus, keeping this barrier in mind different considerations have to be made for different employees. Some of them are very proficient in a certain language, and others will be ok with these languages.

Psychological Barriers-

Various mental and psychological issues may be barriers to effective communication. Some people have stage fear, speech disorders, phobia, and depression. All of these conditions are very difficult to manage sometimes, and will most certainly limit the ease of communication.

Emotional Barriers-

The emotional capacity of a person determines the ease and comfort with which he/she can communicate. An emotionally mature person will be able to communicate effectively. On the other hand, people who let their emotions take over will face certain difficulties. A perfect mixture of emotions and facts is necessary for effective communication. Emotions like anger, frustration and humor can blur the decision-making capacities of a person and thus limit the effectiveness of communication.

Physical Barriers to Communication-

They are the most prominent barriers to effective communication. These barriers are mostly easily removable in principle at least. They include barriers like noise, closed doors, faulty equipment used for communication, closed cabins, etc. Sometimes, in a large offices physical separation between various employees combined with faulty equipment may result in severe barriers to effective communication.

Cultural Barriers-

As the world is getting more and more globalized, any large offices may have people from different parts of the world. Different cultures have

a different meaning for several fundamental values of society. Dressing, religions or lack of them, food, drinks, pets, and general behavior change drastically from one culture to another.

Hence, it is a must that we must take these different cultures into account during communication. This is what we call being culturally appropriate. In many multinational companies, specialized courses are offered at the orientation stages that let people know about other cultures and how to be courteous and tolerant of others.

Organizational Structure Barriers-

As we saw, there are many methods of communication at an organizational level. Each of these methods has its problems and constraints that may become barriers to effective communication. Most of these barriers arise because of misinformation or lack of appropriate transparency available to the employees.

Attitude Barriers-

Certain people like to be left alone. They are the introverts or just people who are not very social. Others like to be social or sometimes extra clingy! Both these cases could become a barrier to communication. Some people have attitude issues, like huge ego and inconsiderate behaviors.

<u>POINTS TO REMEMBER:</u>

- Communication plays an important role in our daily life.
- Powerful communication skills are most needed in today's diverse workplace, and hence the importance of these skills can never be overlooked.
- To achieve effectiveness in communication, one needs to understand the basic of communication. A clear comprehension of the communication process, its fundamentals, and the various channels through which communication flows in an organization is essential to become a successful communicator in any professional setting.
- The act of transferring the ideas from sender to receiver may have various forms.
- There are several different types of communication we are using in our life, whether it is personal or professional.
- Various levels of communications are being used in most of the organizations.
- Different processes are involved in effective communication.

- Barriers to communication must be taken into consideration for making our communication success.
- It is necessary to understand and appropriately deal with the communication failure arising out of certain significant factors. One can enhance communication effectiveness by adhering to the characteristics of effective communication and also by adopting specific strategies for improving communication skills.

GLOSSARY:

- **Communication** It is the passing of information and understanding from one person to another at the same level or different levels.
- **Verbal Communication** It refers to the transfer of information through speaking or sign language. It includes face-to-face, telephone, radio or television and other media. It is mostly used during presentations, video conferences and phone calls, meetings and one-on-one conversations.
- **Non-Verbal Communication** It refers to all unwritten and unspoken messages, both intentional and unintentional. It includes facial expressions, eye contact, and tone of voice, body posture and motions. It may also include the way we wear our clothes or the silence we keep.
- **Encoding** It refers to the process of translating an idea. It is just an idea that came out from the sender mind, and when the sender starts to plan for sending out the message, is the second step of the communication process i.e. planning.
- **Decoding** It refers to the process of translation of symbols encoded by the sender into ideas that can be understood
- **Downward Communication** It refers to the flow of communication from the superiors to subordinates. Information, instructions, directions, and feedback flow in this direction.
- **Upward Communication** It refers to communication flowing from subordinates to superiors. Information, analysis, feedback etc. flow in this direction.
- **Horizontal Communication** It refers to communication among the various divisions of an organization in order to share and coordinate the multifarious activities.
- **Diagonal Communication** It refers to communication that ignores the hierarchical structure and that flows between persons who belong to different levels of hierarchy and who have no direct reporting

relationships.

- **Communication Barriers** It refers to certain factors that may pose problems in the communication process, thereby causing failures in communication.

CHAPTER TWO

NON-VERBAL COMMUNICATION

INTRODUCTION

Communication is the greatest gift of God to mankind. It helps in spinning the wheel of progress as it is through which human beings interact, inform and share their feelings with each other. Communication is simply the act of transferring or exchanging of information by speaking, writing, or using any other semiotic elements. This is fundamental for the survival of human beings and plays a pivotal role in the functioning of an organization irrespective of its size and structure.

OBJECTIVES

After the successful completion of this chapter, you will be able to-

- Understand the concept of Non-Verbal Communication.
- Comprehend the various types of Non-Verbal Communication.
- Realize the importance of Non-Verbal Communication.
- Interpret the Non-Verbal cues effectively.

CONCEPT OF NON-VERBAL COMMUNICATION

Communication, in general, is classified into two types as Verbal Communication and Non- Verbal Communication. Verbal communication is that which is done with the use of words, whereas non-verbal communication is done without the use of words. Non-verbal communication is the oldest means of communication which originated since the existence of human beings. This was the early stage of communication, where man communicated through sounds and symbols. Non-verbal communication includes body language, postures, gestures, glances, etc. It is the vital aspect of the communication process, as a lot of meaning can be conveyed even without uttering a word. Non-verbal communication is a dynamic and effective process where the sender and the receiver use commonly used symbols and codes. For instance, a smile or nodding of the head can convey message lucidly without the use of words.

Importance of non-verbal communication-

Non-Verbal communication is subtle yet more effective than verbal communication. It plays a significant role in the process of communication, as nearly 93% of meaning relies on the non-verbal cues. The rest of the information is conveyed through appearance, postures, tone and facial expressions. Verbal messages are voluntary, which come from the mind and could be manipulated accordingly, while non-verbal signals are involuntary which come from the heart and cannot be controlled consciously. In some cases, this is even more important than the words spoken by an individual. It can have a great impact on the listener and the outcome of the communication. Thus, it conveys the actual attitude and feelings of the sender. Hence, it is vital to recognize the features and importance of non-verbal communication to become a better communicator.

Functions of Non-Verbal Communication-

Non-Verbal communication is strongly related to verbal communication as it reinforces the message conveyed through words. It also serves as a substitute or complement to clarify verbal meaning. This helps one understand the emotional state or the feelings of the communicator. Non-Verbal communication reinforces the relationship between two people and helps them feel more connected. Besides this, subtle non-verbal signals like a smile, nodding of the head, eye contact, etc regulate the flow of communication. There are instances where non-verbal communication is used to contradict the message and thus to indicate the listener that you are sarcastic or not telling the truth.

TYPES OF NON-VERBAL COMMUNICATION

1. Kinesics-

This is also called as body-language and helps us to know the underlying emotions conveyed. In communication, the spoken words state the linguistic or denotative meaning, while the expressions that come along with it reveal the thoughts hidden in the heart.

<u>**Elements of body-language includes-**</u>

- **Facial expressions-** As Adage says, "Action speaks louder than words", human beings can express countless emotions through facial expressions without even saying a word. The face is the most expressive part of the human body. A smile can indicate approval or happiness of a person, while a frown can signal unhappiness or disapproval. Facial expressions are also used to effectively indicate anger, disgust, sadness, surprise, fear, etc. Smile is a powerful communicative signal recognized universally. Smile is infectious and invites an immediate response from the person on the other side. A smile is considered to be genuine when one smiles with the eyes, as the muscles around the eyes are activated, and this cannot be faked. "Human faces are able to make more than 10,000 different expressions, and each one articulates volumes of information with ease."

- **Gestures–** This is nothing but the movement of hands and legs to emphasize the meaning of the spoken words. When a person speaks the words transmits the verbal message, while the body serves as a useful tool to add clarity and effectiveness to the words. Gestures should be convincing and well-timed. It should be natural and spontaneous. The waving of hands or pointing out while arguing expresses our state of mind without even thinking. The use of gestures varies from one culture to the other. The OK sign made with the hand has a positive meaning in English speaking nations while it is considered to be offensive in countries like Germany, Brazil and Russia. Gestures clarify and support the spoken words, and stimulate audience participation as well. Hence, it is important to use these gestures carefully in order to avoid misinterpretation.

- **Postures**– The position of one's body, while speaking, is itself a set of visual messages conveyed to the listener. This indicates if the speaker is nervous, alert or confident in his words. The way a person sits, walks, stands or holds his head, conveys enormous information to the world. Good speaking posture has a positive impact on the audience while postures like slouching or sitting lethargically show a careless attitude of the individual. A person sitting on a chair leaning forward with his head nodding implies that he is open for the discussion. To be an effective and impressive speaker one should hold one's head erect and chin up comfortably. There should be a proper balance of the body with slight natural movement expressing confidence.

- **Eye-contact**– Next to voice, eye contact is the most powerful tool for communicating. Making eye contact with the audience is of prime importance to make them involve and create a sense of personal connection. Looking into one's eyes while speaking shows sincerity and confidence. Speakers who use eye contact are considered to be honest, friendly and skilful. This invokes attentiveness on the part of the audience, which in turn will boost up the confidence of the speaker. Audience unconsciously mirrors the speaker's performance. By gauging the audience reaction, the speaker can alter his words and make it enjoyable. Maintaining eye contact with the listener ensures that what you speak is something important; failing this shows a lack of confidence on the part of the speaker. Eye contact, when used rightly affects to intimidate the opponent, express flirtation and to establish rapport or connection.

- **Haptic**– Haptic is a word derived from the Greek word, which means "I touch". Haptic communication is a branch of communication that deals with the way people and animals communicate through the sense of touch. This is used to express love, care, affection concern, etc. For example, a firm handshake conveys confidence while a warm hug, a patronizing pat on the head shows love and concern, respectively. Human beings, particularly infants, communicate a great deal through touch. New-borns have poorly developed hearing and seeing sense, but they cling to their mother due to the familiarity in their warmth and touch. Touch is the real way to sense the world and is a highly emotional type of communication. It is an effective means to create bonding and strengthening the emotional connection. A warm touch like a handshake, hug, a pat, kiss, etc could bring out the positive outcome, while kicking, pushing, pulling pinching, etc comes under physical abuse. Different cultures have a different interpretation, and hence one should be careful in using this in different cultures. For e.g. Latin Americans greet each other with a long cheek kissing, while in Europeans it is an unconventional means of greeting.

2. *Paralanguage-*

Paralanguage is the voice modulation adopted while we speak. The study of paralanguage is called paralinguistics. Most of the time 'how we speak' matters a lot than what we speak. Words added with combinations of sounds symbolically represent the concept of our communication. The spoken words state the literal meaning, while the way it is said shows the implied meaning. This includes the following-

- **Tone–** Albert Mehrabian a Psychology professor states that the tone of voice influences 38% of the communication. This conveys the type of emotion one carries while speaking. An authoritative tone is used to send across a strict message, influence or persuade, while a light-hearted and a quirky tone is used while speaking to children. The tone is used to express warmth, concern, humour, etc. A compassionate tone creates a great impact on the listener. The tone should be used rightly to express genuine perception, and this makes one stand apart from others.
- **Pitch–** Pitch is the highness or lowness of a person's vocal tone and depends on the number of vibrations per second produced by the vocal cords. This helps in regulating the message and shows the intensity of the message. Greetings or a welcome note has a higher pitch, and a farewell note is better conveyed in a lower pitch.
- **Volume–** Volume expresses the intensity in communication. Generally speaking, a loud voice is considered to be intense while a soft voice or a whispering voice is used to send a covert message or during a flirtatious chat. Volume should be used according to the situation and the relationship with the concerned person. This, when used aptly, enhances the professional image of an individual.
- **Speed of delivery–** This refers to the rate of speech or how fast or slows a person speaks. This plays a prominent role in conveying the emotional

state of a person. When a person speaks very slowly, he may bore the audience, which will divert their attention. On the other hand, a person who speaks at a faster rate may not be comprehendible for the audience. Generally, speed of 120-150 words per minute is recommended and could be beneficial for the audience. This is the normal rate of speed where a speaker could articulate and pronounce his words clearly. Appropriate speed of speech combined with the suitable tone and facial expression can do wonders in the process of communication.

- **Stress and pause** – Stress in oral communication indicates emphasis on a particular word. An important point or message in written communication is denoted by highlighting or underlining it. The same is done by stressing the words in oral communication. Pause is nothing but a small gap given for about a fraction of a second while speaking. This, is in fact, a time given for the audience to assimilate what is said by the speaker. One should know how to use these aspects in the right way to make the speech interesting. Voice varies from person to person. Some may have a pleasant voice, while some people might have a coercive voice. This mainly varies in terms of resonance, tone, pitch, etc. An oral presentation is interesting when the speaker uses proper voice modulation instead of being monotonous. Vocalic cues elaborate or modify verbal and non-verbal meaning by complementing, substituting, regulating or contradicting.

3. Proxemics-

Proxemics is the study of how space and distance between two communicating people influence each other. This has a great deal in indicating the relationship between them. Generally, space influences how people communicate and behave. Less space among people in a crowded area like a train in a rush-hour or a fair in a town, demands a lot of management to adjust the space issues. Whereas an unexpected or a voluntary violation of one's personal space can lead to an adverse reaction. In the first case, at a crowded situation nobody was forced into our personal space, while in the second case, we could sense that someone has violated our personal space. We all have varying definitions of personal space, and this is based on the context and the relationship with the communicating person. Based on this, it is divided into four zones as:

- **Public Zone–** This refers to a space of more than twelve feet away from our body. We maintain this distance in a public place or with a stranger. It is the least personal of the four zones and is used when engaging in a formal address or when a person of high profile like a celebrity or an executive is on the dais. Maintaining such a distance shows power and security reasons could be another aspect. Deep conversation with a person at this level is difficult due to the distance and formality preserved.

- **Social Zone–** Communication in this zone is around four to twelve feet away from the body. This zone is adopted while engaging in casual interaction, with an acquaintance or a colleague. This stands between a public zone and an intimate zone. The expression "Keep someone at arm's length" clearly states that one should be kept out of personal space and should be retained in a professional or social space. This zone is considered to be a safe zone because the possibility of intentional touching, least exists here. In a classroom environment, students and teachers maintain a social zone as this distance is beneficial in acknowledging the presence of every individual student. They are close enough to comprehend every important non-verbal cues and facial expressions.

- **Friendly zone-** This is the zone where the distance is somewhere between two-four feet. Friends, family members, and close acquaintances are entertained in this zone, and most of our communication is under the ambit of the friendly zone. But even in this zone, verbal communication is mostly used to indicate that the presence is not something intimate. This again can be divided as an outer-personal zone which extends from 1.5 – 2 feet distance and an inner-personal zone which comes within a distance of 1.5 feet. In this zone, briefly placing hands on each other's arms or engaging in light social touching to facilitate conversation or feelings of closeness is permissible.

- **Intimate zone–** This is the zone where a person is permitted closer than two feet distance and is reserved only for close friends, family members and intimate people. It is not possible to ignore a person's presence literally when he or she is in this zone, even if we want to. Being close to a person and feeling their physical presence is very comforting than words or verbal communication at the time of distress. Nevertheless, this comes with its own social norms with respect to the amount of closeness that could be displayed in public. There are many situations where our personal space is breached and is more upsetting, even when it is least expected. In such a case, a verbal communication indicating that the closeness is involuntary and unavoidable or non-verbal gestures like crossing our arms or avoiding eye contact will lighten the situation. Hence, it is very crucial to respect others' space in communication for a better relationship.

4. Chronemics-

Chronemics refers to the study of time and its role in communication. Time can be classified into several different categories, including biological, personal, physical, and cultural. A daily cycle that any human being follows like when we eat, sleep, wake up, etc is the natural rhythm or the biological timings of an individual. When this gets disturbed, it affects the mental health and competence of an individual. In the same way, the biological time should be kept in mind while communicating with others as it may cause adverse effects in the communication process. Personal time refers to the ways in which individuals experience time. This is greatly influenced by our mood, our interest level, and other factors. Think about how quickly time passes when you are interested in and therefore engaged in something. Physical time refers to the fixed cycles of days, years, and seasons. Physical time especially seasons, can affect our mood and psychological state. Some people experience seasonal affective disorder that leads them to experience emotional distress and anxiety during the changes of seasons, primarily from warm and bright to dark and cold (summer to fall and winter). Cultural time refers to how a large group of people view time and its influences on social realities and how we interact with others.

Besides, the way we utilize time shows our personality and status to a certain extent. Executives and celebrities may run consistently behind schedule, making others wait for them. Promptness and the amount of time that is socially acceptable for lateness and waiting vary among individuals and contexts. But maintaining punctuality and handling time effectively portrays a positive image of oneself.

5. Artifactual–

This denotes the meaning conveyed by the physical appearance of a person and the external setting of a place. Physical characteristics include the body shape, weight height, attractiveness and the way a person dresses himself or herself. This unconsciously sends a message about a person's interest in taking care of oneself, fashion quotient, etc. Although it is not always right to judge a book by its cover to a certain extent, a physically attractive person has distinct advantages in many aspects of life. This has resulted in, attracting people's interest in health and beauty, dieting, gym, etc. It is generally said 'Dress yourself as you expect to be treated'. But one should remember the fact that attractiveness varies from culture to culture. This sends religious faith or cultural symbols. For example, white colour is considered to be special and used in formal or special occasions in the Western culture, while in Indian context, it is worn during mourning or funeral ceremony and is considered inauspicious. This does not pertain only to accessories like jewels, clothes, hairstyle, etc but also to the shape or physical stature of an individual.

Secondly, talking about the physical set up of a place or environment itself sends a subtle message on the quality of a person dwelling in that place. The standard of furniture, their arrangement, the lighting of the place in an office environment conveys the designation of the person occupying the room. To sum-up, artifactual communication expresses the status of a person which defines the roles within relationships.

6. Silence-

Silence, as said by Abraham Lincoln; "The more a man speaks, the less he is understood", silence is one of the most powerful communication tools. But this is widely underutilized by many persons. The context of a situation better determined the power of silence. At workplace what we speak is always not important, but the non-verbal signals communicate a great deal of message to our colleagues. This, in fact, has a great impact on one's career prospects. Silence is laden with meaning and can make or break a relationship. A constructive silence indicates respect, empathy and encourages a speaker, thus deepening the understanding between the two parties. Sometimes silence is uncomfortable, embarrassing and destructively happens to be a barrier in communication. People in higher position use silence to strengthen their power and maintain their stature. For instance, an interviewer uses silence as a tool to check how the candidate conducts himself or herself.

VERBAL VS. NON-VERBAL COMMUNICATION

Verbal communication is where the sender uses words, technology and other social media to convey or transmit messages. In contrast, non-verbal communication is where messages are conveyed through body language, gestures, vocalic elements and other environmental factors. Verbal communication is done consciously and could be altered or manipulated according to the need and hence not reliable in all situations. Non-verbal communication is an involuntary action and comes spontaneously, thus taken to be more reliable comparatively. In the case of verbal communication, we use a structured pattern which could be understood immediately, and quick feedback is possible. At the same time, non-verbal cues depend on the context, and one should have a mastery over it to interpret it rightly.

INTERPRETING NON-VERBAL CUES

Non-verbal communication plays a predominant role in communication, and hence it is essential to learn how to use and interpret it for effective communication. Non-verbal communications should reinforce the spoken words. In order to have a better understanding of non-verbal communication, one should have the ability to listen with your eyes and ears, and pay attention to people's posture, hand movements and eye contact. Interpreting gestures, facial expressions and posture allows us to have a sneak peek into a person's true emotional status. Such insight can give you a definite advantage on the job. Review the basics of body language then observe the emotional signals that others give off long before any words are spoken. One can become proficient in mastering the ability to read other people's body language by practice. Expertise in interpreting will also give you more confidence and skill in handling social and business interactions in an effective way.

ROLE OF NON-VERBAL COMMUNICATION IN INTERVIEW

Non-verbal communication, like body language and facial expressions, play a vital role at the time of interviews. The first impression about a person is formed mostly based on the body language, and the actual verbal content has a meagre role in it. In short, it is 'Action speaks louder than words.' Professionally dressing oneself way with neatly groomed hair and a formal outfit is what is needed to create a first visual impression with the interviewer. The documents and testimonies which you carry should be arranged professionally in a proper portfolio. After entering the company, a polite and professional approach should be adopted. During the time of interview, the sitting posture should be proper. One should sit straight and avoid slouching at the same time, appear natural and confident. Avoid fidgeting with your pen or anything else. Make proper eye contact, be polite and keep an even tone in your speech. Listen carefully and do not interrupt when the interviewer is speaking. Non-verbal communication has a significant role in making or breaking a job opportunity.

POWER OF Non-VERBAL COMMUNICATION IN PRESENTATION & GROUP DISCUSSIONS

Non-verbal communication is a very powerful mode of communication which has a prominent role in determining the success of an individual during group discussions and interviews. During a presentation, when a speaker walks up the stage with a big smile and greets the audience in a pleasant and a confident way looking into their eyes sets the tone for the rest of the speaking time. Even before he started speaking, he has connected with the audience and built up a friendly atmosphere. When a speaker makes eye contact with the audience, he shows his level of confidence and engages the audience. Facial expressions are also a reflection of emotions and add voluminous meaning to the spoken words. Posture or the way a person stands while giving a presentation is another important aspect to govern. One should stand straight with the body weight evenly distributed on both the feet. Leaning on the podium, rocking from side to side or putting your hands into pockets, unconsciously conveys one's lethargic attitude. Paralinguistic elements like tone, volume, stress & pause are aspects which make the speech interesting and worth hearing. Maintaining an even tone throughout tends to make a speech boring. So, it is important to change the voice modulation to grab the attention of the audience.

During a group discussion, using non-verbal communication like nodding one's head or waving hands can effectively demonstrate agreement or disagreement to some point. Not making eye contact shows your lack of attentiveness and distracted mind. Tone and pitch should be used properly to set the right tone of the discussion. The face is the most expressive part of the body and when used in the right way can convey all kind of emotions like happiness, fear, consent panic, etc. As one cannot speak throughout the discussion involvement could be demonstrated through non-verbal gestures. Your words and body language should complement each other. A group discussion is a situation where there is an amalgamation of verbal and non-verbal communication which varies from person to person, culture to culture and context to context. Using the right kind of non-verbal cues can aid in building a good rapport with the counterparts and smooth flow of the discussion. A right mix of verbal and non-verbal communication sends the messages in a better way leading to a better perception of what is being said. Non-verbal communication reflects an individual's personality and professional stance.

POINTS TO REMEMBER:

Non-verbal communication is the message passed on to the listener without the usage of words. This is symbolic and includes elements like body language, facial expressions, gestures postures etc. Non-verbal communication is an art and mastering the technique doesn't happen overnight and will demand an increasing self-awareness. Understanding these cues is important not only for the speaker but also for the interpreter. Non-verbal communication can take various forms, each of which illustrates or replaces a certain part of the verbal communication, and it depends on the context. One needs to be intelligent, intellectually and emotionally to assimilate non-verbal cues in the right way. And once you've gotten hold of your non-verbal communication, it'll be an indispensable skill that can definitely ensure credibility and success in your profession.

GLOSSARY:

- **Non-Verbal communication**- is subtle yet more effective than verbal communication.
- **Kinesics**- also called as body language, helps us know the underlying emotions conveyed.
- **Gestures**– is the movement of hands and legs to emphasize the meaning of the spoken words.

- **Postures–** the position of one's body, while speaking, is itself a set of visual messages conveyed to the listener.
- **Haptic–** is a word derived from the Greek word which means "I touch". Haptic communication is a branch of communication that deals with the way people and animals communicate through the sense of touch.
- **Paralanguage-** is the voice modulation adopted while we speak. The study of paralanguage is called paralinguistic.

CHAPTER THREE

LISTENING SKILLS

INTRODUCTION

Communication skills have a great impact on the success of an individual. A person's ability to stand apart from his counterparts is often determined by his communication skills and proficiency in English language. In order to be a well-rounded communicator, one should be proficient in Listening, Speaking, Reading and Writing (LSRW) the foundation skills of language learning. All these four skills go hand in hand and should be learnt and practiced in parallel. Speaking and Writing are said to be productive or active processes, as here an individual comes out with the output of ideas and uses language. Listening and Reading are receptive or passive processes, as one receives ideas and does not involve producing of words, phrases or sentences. Mastering these skills is essential for personal as well as professional betterment of an individual in this competitive world.

OBJECTIVES

After the successful completion of this chapter, you will be able to-

- Understand the importance of listening skills.
- Assimilate the differences between listening and hearing
- Adopt simple techniques to ensure effective listening.
- Realize the vitality of listening as an interpersonal skill
- Listening strategies for better comprehension

LISTENING PROCESS

What is Listening skill?

Listening is receiving sounds through ears and identifying the speech sounds. Listening is the ability to pay attention and understand the communicated information and providing appropriate feedback. Listening is the key to effective communication, without which messages can be misunderstood. It seems to be a natural activity but an essential skill that has to be mastered. Listening is a receptive process which demands a lot of attentiveness.

<u>Listening Process-</u>

Process means a series of actions involved to complete a task successfully. Listening is a process which involves receiving sounds and interpreting them into meaningful words. This involves five stages in order to understand and retain what we hear fully.

- **Receiving** – This is an intentional focus on the sounds produced by a speaker. Here the listener receives or hears the sounds through his ears. This is the response caused by the sound waves which stimulates the sensory receptors of the ear.
- **Understanding/Interpreting** - This is the stage where we attempt to attach meaning to the words received. Here the sound received by the ear reaches the brain, and the sounds are deciphered into meaningful words of a language. Understanding the words depends on the background, experience and accent of the speaker. This also depends on our perceptions and prior experience with the concerned speaker. For example, advice given by a person can be taken in the right sense by his close friend, but an acquaintance or a colleague may not necessarily take it positively. Instead, he could be annoyed and take it to be sarcastic. For better interpersonal relationship, a listener must understand the intended meaning of the speaker along with the context.
- **Remembering** – Remembering is an important stage of the listening process, which shows the listener has not only heard the sounds but also has interpreted the sounds and stored it like words in the brain. Day-

to-day messages or communication is easy to understand while a highly complex message or a new concept demands greater listening skill. Here, the comprehended message is absorbed and stored to facilitate future recall.

- **Evaluating** – The fourth stage of the listening process is evaluating or analyzing the received message. This evaluation again can vary from one person to the other. Messages are positively evaluated if the speaker speaks clearly in a convincing way with valid data and a positive body language rather than being rude and authoritative. Personal opinions or prejudices also have a role in evaluating one's message. It is always better to refrain from making judgments and to focus on the message of the speaker.
- **Responding** – Responding also referred to as the feedback is the final stage of the communication process. This is where the listener shows his involvement or participation in the communication process. Any signal given verbally or non-verbally is considered to be feedback from the listener. For example, after a lecture in a classroom, if the students come up with some doubts or questions for clarification, it is a positive response. While the same students trying to leave the lecture room immediately is considered to be a negative sign.

IMPORTANCE OF LISTENING SKILLS

Listening plays an important role in the process of communication and is a vital skill needed in every walk of life. While we listen, we build trust and a healthy relationship with the speaker. In the era of high-tech communication, we should listen to one another whenever possible, as one really gets rare opportunities and time to have a discussion or a conversation. When we listen to others, we get to know about the skill of speaking, style of framing arguments and the art of presenting facts. This will enable us to improve our vocabulary skill and oratory skills. Listening intently avoids misinterpretation and reduces the risk of misunderstanding. When a person listens he happens to know the opinion of others and explore a new horizon of ideas leading to personal development. While paying keen attention and interest to what others speak, unconsciously we convey to them that their message is important. This paves the way for better prospects in team-based work culture.

DIFFERENCE BETWEEN HEARING AND LISTENING

Hearing is a natural ability of a person and an involuntary process where the brain automatically responds to the sound that goes on in the surroundings, and it needs no effort. This is a physiological process where the vibrations produced by sounds reach the eardrums. Hearing does not require concentration, and we do not have any control over any sounds which we hear. Listening, on the other hand, is a voluntary, diligent and a purposeful action done by a person. This is the process of paying thoughtful attention and giving consideration to the sounds or spoken words. Listening is where we set aside ourselves and be mindful of other's words.

For example, while standing on a railway platform, we happen to hear different sounds like the coming of the train, birds chirping, a baby crying and the porters yelling. These sounds come to us automatically, and we don't pay effort to listen to them, this is called hearing. On the other hand, amidst various noises, we pay a conscious effort to the announcement made about the train which we are to board. Thus, listening is a conscious psychological process.

TYPES OF LISTENING

Listening is not a skill that just happens, it needs a conscious effort to nurture and develop it. The way we pay attention to what people say shows the relationship with the individual.

- **Active Listening-** Active listening is where full concentration is paid to what the speaker is saying. Here there is a deep engagement with the speaker and this is expressed through several verbal and non-verbal cues. This could be particularly observed in a classroom atmosphere. Active listening is very important for students and has several positive outcomes. This means listening with all senses and can be acquired and developed with practice. Non-verbal clues like maintaining an eye-contact, nodding your head, giving a smile, etc could indicate your interest and encourage the speaker. A posture like leaning slightly forward also shows attentiveness on the part of the listener. Verbal indications like remembering the name of the speaker, idea or the concepts conveyed during the previous conversation is an encouraging factor. Raising questions is another aspect which not only shows the concentration of the listener but also his interest in clarifying doubts and widening the knowledge. Reflection is another method where the message is nearly repeated by paraphrasing the message said by the speaker and demonstrating interest and understanding. Summarizing is another technique in which the main points of the message are reiterated logically. Engagement with the speaker could be done in any of these methods. Lack of these signals could dissuade the speaker or make him feel that he is boring. Active listening is a process which demands patience, practice and motivation to listen. People from varied fields like leaders, entrepreneurs, students, managers need to practice active listening for effective communication.

- **Comprehensive listening-** In Comprehensive listening, we pay attention to comprehend or understand the message delivered by the speaker. This involves the use of cognitive skills and is based on one's knowledge and perception. It eventually varies from person to person. For better comprehensive listening, we should have good vocabulary skills, for this one should be active and focused on interpreting the main idea of the speaker. Listening to television news or attending a lecture may be an example of a comprehensive listening.

- **Discriminative Listening-** This is the basic form of listening, where much attention is not paid in interpreting the words. Here, the listener discriminates or distinguishes the sounds of the words spoken by the speaker. In this type, the prime focus is paid to the paralinguistic cues like accents, stress, pronunciation of words, etc. For example, when a baby hears someone speaking, it first pays attention to distinguish or identify its mother's voice. It does not have the ability to understand the meaning of the words, but it listens to the sound just to make out who the speaker is. This is also adopted by non- native speakers of a language. Such type of listening helps us understand the mood of the speaker when keen attention is paid to the tone. As we grow by age, we develop the ability to identify the subtle differences in the way sounds are made or words are pronounced. These subtleties make us understand if the person who is speaking is happy or sad. This type of listening combined with visual stimuli like body language helps one to comprehend the message rightly in every aspect.

- **Critical Listening-** Critical listening is where the speaker listens understands and evaluates the message by analysing it. Since the message received is judged, it is an intellectual process and demands a deep concentration and understanding of what is said. Psychiatrist, lawyers and people adopt this type of listening in the business field, education sector, etc where they grasp the points immediately and keep it streamlined and efficient. By being critical in listening it enables one to scan through the vitality of message which enables in the quick decision-making process and quicker analysis of the problem. Critical listening is a skill greatly needed in highly stressful situations and things related to finance. etc. One needs to master the art of critical listening and critical thinking to scrutinize the fact amidst several opinions and exaggerations. Separating facts from opinion is vital to judging the quality of evidence. When a person develops the ability to think rationally, he can understand the logical connections between ideas reflect on one's own beliefs and systematically solve problems. Here one should understand the message along with its context and consequently evaluate the message.

- **Appreciative Listening**- Appreciative listening is listening for pleasure or enjoyment. This is where the listener is active to information or facts which he is interested in. It may be anything that helps a person to achieve his goal or something entertaining. We use appreciative listening while listening to good music, motivational speech, poetry or anything pertaining to one's interest. This again varies from person to person according to the individual's perception. It also depends on factors like presentation and previous experience. For instance, a motivational speaker on the stage creates an impact on the audience not only by his speech but also by his personality, voice and delivery style which entrances the listener. On the other hand, if we have encountered a bitter experience with the same speaker, whatever he says will be looked upon in a biased manner, unappreciatively. Appreciative listening is essential for partnerships or to make any relationship work.

- **Sympathetic listening**- Sympathetic listening is listening with sympathy, showing involvement and attempting to show understanding, compassion and support. When someone from our friend's circle or a close family member is in a difficult situation like a loss in business or separation from a dear one, we use this type of listening to show our concern for them. Here the listener tries to show that he understands the pain of the speaker and what he is going through. This is better conveyed through suitable body language accompanied by the verbal message. Being a good listener helps the other person relax and have confidence in you.

- **Empathetic Listening-** Empathetic listening is where one tries to understand the problem of the other person by placing oneself in the shoes of the other. In this type, the listener tries to understand the situation by raising a series of questions which will bring several factors to light. This is the highest degree of understanding not as an observer but experiencing the feelings ourselves. In a close relationship, feeling others pain or pleasure is a great sign of love or care for them. Empathetic listening is also called as therapeutic listening, where the listener, like a therapist, tries to bring the speaker out of the situation by the way of counselling, or advising without being judgmental.

BARRIERS TO EFFECTIVE LISTENING

A barrier, in general, is something which stops or interprets the free flow of a process. Barrier in the process of communication results in misunderstandings leading to drastic consequences at times. Barriers in listening could be in two forms as:

Environmental or Physical Barrier-

A physical barrier is the environmental condition that acts as a barrier in the process of listening. This includes noise in any form or distance. Noise is any unwanted sound which causes a great disturbance and reduces the effectiveness of communication. It becomes difficult to pay attention in a noisy surrounding. When the speaker is speaking over a phone and there arises a problem in the network, it causes disturbances in the flow of communication. Similarly, unpleasant atmosphere or improper lighting creates uncomfortable feelings and disrupts the attention of the listener, thus acting as a barrier. Information overflow is another barrier which strains the listener from paying constant attention.

Psychological barrier or Cognitive Barrier-

A psychological barrier is the psychological influence or state of mind, which creates an obstacle and prevents the listener from paying attention to what is said. This noise that stems out from our psychological state of mind can impede the listening process. State of mind has a great impact in influencing the communication process. If a listener is not in a good state of mind or is angry, his listening and interpreting ability gets blurred. Hence whatever he listens is understood according to his mood, and thereby, he fails to take the message in its actual sense. Perception is the mindset of the person which decides the interpretation of a message.

Attitude is the established way of understanding, and this also depends on previous experience encountered with the concerned speaker. If we don't have a cordial relationship with the speaker, obviously there arises a barrier in our mind which prevents us from paying attention to the speaker. This results in misunderstanding as the view of the person is already set. Some people tend to jump to conclusions without involving active listening or resort to selective listening. This ultimately lowers the morale of the speaker. Emotions such as anger, nervousness, restlessness, etc also have a role in listening and communication process.

Prejudice is another preconceived opinion or feeling, which is irrational and dangerous. A prejudiced person makes less effort to listen or understand. However, this barrier can be overcome by making a conscious effort to have control over one's thoughts, by being in the present and respecting knowledge and skills of the person irrespective of their background.

STRATEGIES TO LISTEN EFFECTIVELY

For effective communication, listening skill plays a key role at various levels of any profession or organization. Poor listening skills make a great negative impact and reduces productivity and thus results in conflicts and misunderstandings between the speaker and the listener. What employers look for in a person is not only hard skills but also the soft skills, which includes communication, interpersonal skills, emotional intelligence, etc. Listening skill is a part of soft skill and is of great demand in service industries like education, banking, health, etc. Good listening skill, like any other ability, comes by practice and can be honed by putting in conscious effort.

- **Desire to listen** - The first step is that a person should be prepared mentally and desirous to listen to the speaker. The focus should be on the speaker without any distractions and concentrate on the message that is communicated.

- **Listen without interrupting** – When somebody is speaking, one should listen without disturbing him by asking questions in-between. Once he has finished, his speech then any clarification could be made. In short, listen to respond not to react.
- **Put the speaker at ease**- Audience plays a vital role in putting the speaker at ease and encouraging them to come out with their best ideas in the best way possible. Non- verbal signals like maintaining eye-contact reveal your interest in the speech.
- **Avoid distractions** – When a person is speaking, avoid behaviours like fidgeting with the pen, checking mobiles or looking out through the window indicates that you are bored with the speech.
- **Prevent mind wandering** - This is an important distraction where people with untrained mind get easily distracted by random objects or inner thoughts.
- **Be Open-minded** – Try to listen without judging or being critical of what the other person is speaking. Do not try to justify your thoughts or beliefs and try to be patient without trying to jump into a conclusion.
- **Empathize** – Try to understand the message from the speaker's point of view. This can avoid being judgmental. Set aside filters and listen to understand.
- **Take notes** – Importance of writing or taking notes cannot be denied. While taking notes, we create a permanent record of what is being said besides reinforcing the message. It is evident enough to show the interest of the listener.
- **Listen to the tone and emotions** – Paralinguistic elements like tone and volume amplify the emotions and convey a lot about the feeling of the person. This can help us to connect better with the speaker.

LISTENING AS A VITAL COMPONENT OF INTERPERSONAL SKILLS

Interpersonal skill is the ability to communicate socializes and builds relationship with others. This is also called as 'People skills' and includes the innate personality of a person to handle a social situation. Effective interpersonal skills are vital for career advancement and are an asset to steer through change and daily tasks. This includes active listening, teamwork, responsibility, leadership quality, patience, empathy, etc to name a few.

Importance of listening in a relationship is quintessential. Listening or Active Listening is the process where a person listens to others to gather information and connect with the speaker. In this type, the listener avoids any kind of distraction and honestly tries to assimilate what is being said. Listening is done for a variety of reasons like, some people listen to learn, to be informed, or to get entertained and it depends upon the context of the communication. In relationship, we listen empathetically, as at some point of time everyone wants to vent out their feelings and problems to someone who will listen. We also listen to understand a person who is attempting to speak emotionally, and intellectually. Listening is of two types, where one listens to understand and the other is where one listens to respond. In cases, where people listen to understand the relationship is smoother and cordial. Active and empathetic listening is the life of any relationship. When we pay heed to other people, they feel respected, cared and often less defensive. By listening we convey our concern to them. Good listeners are less judgmental and provide a safe environment for the speakers. Active listening is a cornerstone of any relationship and cultivates intimacy when combined with empathy. This means that we are fully present and reflective on how we listen to the person. The person who speaks does not want a solution always, but they need someone to listen with humility and empathy. Human being always has a tendency to be seen, heard and understood in a relationship. A little bit of active listening from time to time profoundly nourishes the relationship.

POINTS TO REMEMBER:

- Listening is a vital part of the communication process and is one of the four skills of the language.
- It is a receptive procedure where a person pays attention to what others say and try to infer meaning out of it. This complex skill can be developed through constant practice.
- Listening process includes the action of receiving the message, comprehending it, remembering, evaluating, and then responding.
- Generally speaking, there are eight types of listening, and this depends on the context and purpose of the listener.
- At times there arises a number of obstacles that stand in the way of effective listening, called barriers. These could be skilfully overcome by

engaging in active listening and being in the present moment.

- Keeping an open mind and avoid being judgmental is crucial for effective communication. By preparing ourselves to be a good listener, we can become a good communicator.

GLOSSARY:

- Listening is receiving sounds through ears and identifying the speech sounds. Listening is the ability to pay attention and understand the communicated information and providing appropriate feedback.
- Listening plays an important role in the process of communication and is a vital skill needed in every walk of life.
- Active listening is where full concentration is paid to what the speaker is saying. Here there is a deep engagement with the speaker, and this is expressed through several verbal and non-verbal cues.
- Comprehensive listening, we pay attention to comprehend or understand the message delivered by the speaker.
- Discriminative Listening is the basic form of listening, where much attention is not paid in interpreting the words.
- Critical Listening is where the speaker listens, understands and evaluates the message by analysing it.
- Appreciative listening is listening for pleasure or enjoyment. This is where the listener is active to information or facts which he is interested in.
- Sympathetic listening is listening with sympathy, showing involvement and attempting to show understanding, compassion and support.
- Empathetic listening is where one tries to understand the problem of the other person by placing oneself in the shoes of the other.
- A physical barrier is the environmental condition that acts as a barrier in the process of listening. This includes noise in any form or distance.

CHAPTER FOUR

READING SKILLS

INTRODUCTION

Reading basically is a physical process of comprehending a text using your very important sense organ "Eyes". However, reading becomes studying when it is done with the involvement of all the mental strength, concentration, comprehension, and analysis. Studying involves the practices of answering questions, note-making, summarizing, reading the text more than once, and analysing the written words thoroughly.

In short, we can say to study is to read, observe or to know the information in depth. A study of the major types of reading skills may assist you in improving reading comprehension as well as in employing the required skill for different reading situations. The skills used while reading includes Scanning /previewing, skimming, intensive reading, extensive reading identifying, and sequencing.

OBJECTIVES

After successful completion of this chapter, you will be able to-

- Understand the mechanics of reading.
- Preview the text with the techniques discussed.
- Define and differentiate between skimming and scanning.
- Identify the context.
- Sequence the sentences with perfect comprehension skills.

PREVIEWING

Previewing means surveying a text quickly before, you read it carefully. You preview when you want to get information. Previewing can help you with your reading. When you preview, you get an idea about the content, this way, your brain which is already activate gets an idea about the context and helps you in understanding the subject matter of the text.

For Example: You might preview by-

- A newspaper, by reading headlines
- A letter, by looking at its envelope
- A book, by reading its front and back cover The previewing can help you to decide-
- Which article to read
- Whether to open a letter or not (It can be a junk mail).
- If the book is worth reading or buying.

Why use previewing?

According to research, previewing a text can improve comprehension (Graves, Cooke, & LaBerge, 1983, cited in Paris et al., 1991). Previewing a text helps readers prepare for what they are about to read and set a purpose for reading. Previewing helps students become more active and powerful readers. By activating prior knowledge and making connections, students are thinking about big ideas. They can predict and infer, looking for text evidence to support their lines of thinking.

The genre determines the reader's methods for previewing-

- Readers preview nonfiction to find out what they know about the subject and what they want to find out. It also helps them understand how an author has organized information.
- Readers preview biography to determine something about the person in the biography, the time period, some possible places, and events in the life of the person.
- Readers preview fiction to determine characters, setting, and plot. They also preview to make predictions about story's problems and solutions.

Previewing Techniques-

Consider previewing a text as similar to watching a movie preview. Think of previewing a text as similar to creating a movie trailer. A successful preview for either a movie or a reading experience will capture what the overall work is going to be about, generally what expectations the audience can have of the experience to come, how the piece is structured, and what kinds of patterns will emerge.

Previewing engages your prior experience, and asks you to think about what you already know about the subject matter, or the author, or the publication. Then anticipate what new information might be ahead of you when you return to read this text more closely. In order to preview anything certain steps need to be kept in mind:

- Look at the title, subtitles, author, and source try to guess what the text is about.
- Read the introductory paragraph.
- Consider what you already know about the topic.
- Look at the visuals.
- If you are reading in a foreign language, try and predict which economic terms and general expressions might appear in the text.

How to use previewing?

When readers preview a text before they read, they first ask themselves whether the text is a fiction or non-fiction. If the text is fiction or biography, readers look at the title, chapter headings, introductory notes, and illustrations for a better understanding of the content and possible settings or events.

If the text is non-fiction, readers look at text features and illustrations (and their captions) to determine the subject matter and to recall prior knowledge, to decide what they know about the subject. Previewing also helps readers figure out what they don't know and what they want to find out.

SKIMMING

It is a method of reading a text rapidly in order to get the basic overall idea. For instance, many people skim read a newspaper article just to get a quick overview. Skimming is generally used to identify the main ideas of the text quickly. Skimming is done at speed three to four times faster than normal reading. Skimming is done when one has to read a lot of material in a limited duration of time. It is used when one wants to see if an article may be of interest in one's research.

Skimming is done to gain a general impression of whether the text is of any use to you or not. You can see people skimming through books in a bookstore before they decide to buy them. You need not necessarily search for a specific item or keyword, and many parts of the material may be left unread. The purpose of skimming is to get a gist, and check the relevance, grasp its central theme and the main points. It prepares you for the more concentrated effort of detailed reading, which is to follow if the text is useful.

Example-

A learner taking a reading exam decides to approach the text by looking at the title, introductions, and any diagrams and sub-headings, then skim read to get a clear general idea of what the text is about.

In the classroom, skimming is a specific reading skill which is common in reading newspapers, messages, and e-mails. Learners must understand that there is no need to read every word when skimming, so often teachers set this as a timed task to encourage speed.

In general, how to skim?

- Read the title.
- Read the introduction or the first paragraph.
- Read the first sentence of every other paragraph.
- Read any headings and sub-headings.
- Notice any pictures, charts, or graphs.
- Notice any italicized or boldface words or phrases.
- Read the summary or last paragraph.

Steps to Skim through a book-

- Title: Read the title carefully
- Subtitle: Some titles are ambiguous, but subtitles tend to shed more light so carefully read the subtitle.

- Read the preface: In preface, the author explains exactly what the book is all about, so this step need not be skipped.
- Look at the table of contents: Table of contents gives information on the book's subject structure and components.
- Read the publisher's blurb: Publisher's blurb usually located in the back; some are found in the books dust cover. This too is an excellent way to discover the gist of a book.
- Identification of chapters: Identify the important chapters to be read.
- Topics of the chapter: Read the first and the last lines of each paragraph to get a feel for the flow of argument and the topics of the chapter.

Steps to skim a general text-

- Look at the title, subheadings, pictures, diagrams and whatever else stands out on the page. Turn the subheadings into questions in your mind.
- Read the first and last paragraph of the chapter. These paragraphs introduce and wrap up the chapter. And contain keep information that can be important to remember.
- Read the first sentence of each paragraph. Try to restate what you read in your own words. You can either write it down or say it out loud. This reiteration will implant the subject material you are skimming in your head.
- Try to read the text quickly, but pay attention to what you pick up in the process. Focus on the nouns and verbs. These are considered keywords and will help you in getting a general sense of what the author is discussing.

SCANNING

It is reading something rapidly for some specific piece of information. You can use this skill when you are in search of keywords. It is a method one often uses when looking up a word in the telephone book or dictionary. One search for keywords or ideas. In most cases, one knows what one is looking for, so one concentrates in finding a particular answer. Scanning involves moving one's eyes quickly down the page seeking specific words and phrases. Scanning is also used when one finds a resource to determine whether it will answer to one's question. Once one has scanned the document, one might go and skim it.

Scanning is a reading technique to be used when you want to find specific information quickly. In scanning, you have a question in your mind, and you read a passage only to find the answer, ignoring unrelated information.

Example-

Scanning a telephone book or dictionary to look for a name or a word- You see every item on the page, but you don't necessarily read all the pages –you skip anything you are not looking for. You just have to concentrate on the keyword and need not recall the exact content of the page. Scanning saves times, but it has to be done with accuracy. This skill develops with practice.

How to Scan?

- State the specific information you are looking for.
- Try to anticipate how the answer will appear and what clues you might use to help you locate the answer. For example, if you were looking for a certain date, you would quickly read the paragraph looking only for numbers.
- Use headings and any other aids that will help you identify which sections might contain the information you are looking for.
- Selectively read and skip through sections of the passage.

Scanning is basically skimming with a more tightly focused purpose. Skimming to locate a particular fact or figure, or to see whether the text mentions a subject you're researching. Scanning is essential in the writing of research papers, when you may need to look through many articles and books in order to find the material you need. Keep a specific set of goals in mind as you scan the text, and avoid becoming distracted by other material. You can note what you'd like to return to later when you do have time to read further and use scanning to move ahead in your research project.

When to use scanning?

As convenient as it seems, skimming can't guarantee you all the important points. Usually, you need scanning when you find a friend's phone number in a telephone book or last night football scores in the newspaper. Or when you're in a new restaurant knowing they have your favourite dish but not sure the price is reasonable; you also need to scan along the menu to see it with the price. Scanning significantly proves its value when researching and studying. These two kinds of activity can't be successful if they depend on only your general knowledge.

You may also need scanning to locate the correct answer for given questions. You are likely to scan when you have no intention of getting a general idea. Obviously, if you have no doubt of your purposes for reading, and other unrelated information is far from support, now take scanning into your consideration. Scanning is perfect when it comes to looking for something more particular rather than an overview idea in your mind.

Skimming and Scanning are close friends-

Despite all the differences between skimming and scanning, those two friends seem to be best together. They have been taught in almost every class of reading method. This is because of the fact that practising either of them can show great results.

However, the combination of skimming and scanning is even much greater. It's like insurance for your fast reading: you read quicker, but you don't miss out anything important. Why and how can these techniques do such an amazing job? Skimming takes the role of covering the whole reading material to assure you get what's beneficial and leave out the useless ones. Scanning plays a part in taking out the most precious facts you need. It's a responsible way of fast reading that no one could deny.

IDENTIFYING THE TOPIC SENTENCES

The topic sentence is the main point, or main idea of a paragraph. The topic sentence should identify the main idea and point of the paragraph. To choose an appropriate topic sentence, read the paragraph, and think about its main idea and point. The supporting details in the paragraph (the sentences other than the topic sentence) will develop or explain the topic sentence.

A topic sentence essentially tells readers what the rest of the paragraph is about. For example, if the topic sentence concerns the types of endangered species that live in the ocean, then every sentence after that needs to expound on that subject. Topic sentences also need to relate back to the thesis of the essay. If you cannot identify the topic sentence of a paragraph, your comprehension will suffer since you will not be able to understand the author's main idea.

<u>The following four steps will help you identify the topic sentence-</u>

Step 1. Find the topic of the paragraph-

Do not confuse the topic with the topic sentence. The topic is simply the who or what being discussed in the paragraph, while the topic sentence includes the topic and the point being made about it. Knowing the topic will point you towards the topic sentence. Circle the words used most often in the paragraph. Also, circle any synonyms or pronoun references.

Step 2. Identify the keywords that signal a topic sentence-

While not all topic sentences include keywords, when you come across sentences with any of these phrases, you can be fairly certain that it is the topic sentence.

Step 3. Identify the major details-

Sometimes, the supporting details are easier to find than the topic sentence. If so, identify all major details, and see what they have in common. This is an especially effective technique for paragraphs that do not have an explicitly stated topic sentence.

Step 4. Look beyond the first sentence to identify the topic sentence-

Do not assume that the topic sentence is the first sentence of the paragraph. In most paragraphs, the topic sentence is one of the first sentences; however, that is not always the case. Sometimes, the writer includes some introductory material before getting to the point, or the writer sums up the major details with a topic sentence at the end.

Classification and types of topic sentences-

Topic Sentence is usually the first sentence and introduces the main idea, whereas sometimes introduces the details.

Types of Topic Sentences-

1. General Topic Sentence-

Names the main idea of the paragraph. Not specific. Examples of a General Topic Sentence

The hot trend in advertising these days is to hire real, live stars. Kevin James would have been 20 years old this September.

2. Clueing Topic Sentence-

Names the main idea of the paragraph. This type of topic sentence gives a "clue" about the details of the paragraph. This type gives a "hint" about what the paragraph is about! Examples of a Clueing Topic Sentence are-

The four seasons spice up our lives.

Tents come in a variety of shapes and sizes.

The citizens of Lawrence have several reasons for building a new high school.

3. Specific Topic Sentence-

Names the main idea of a paragraph, but names the specific details to be covered in order. Example of Specific Topic Sentences-

Air pollution is caused by vehicles and industries.

Charles Darwin lived an interesting life as an explorer, writer, and scientist.

Diseases caused by vitamin deficiencies are beriberi, pellagra, and scurvy, and rickets.

INFERRING LEXICAL AND CONTEXTUAL MEANING

Lexical meanings are actual meanings, meanings that are following the results of our sensory observations, or meaning as they are, while contextual meanings are the meanings of a lexeme or words that are in one context.

In communicating between speakers and speech partners sometimes misunderstandings occur. This is because there are differences in the messages conveyed so that the meaning of the language expressed by the speaker is not in accordance with the response of the listener. The difference in response to meaning can occur because a word or a sentence can have several meanings. Tarigan (1995: 11-13) generally divides meaning into two types, namely linguistic meaning and social (cultural) meaning. Then the linguistic meaning is divided into lexical meanings and structural meanings, as well as referential meanings and precedential meanings. In line with Tarigan, Heatherington (1980: 135-136), as quoted by Tarigan (1995: 11-12), also divides meaning into two namely, lexical meaning and lexico-structural meaning.

Furthermore, the lexical meaning is divided into denotative meanings and connotative meanings, literal meanings and figurative meanings. The meanings associated with morphemes and words are called lexical meanings (Chaer, 2012: 45).

Lexical meanings are actual meanings, meanings that are in accordance with the results of our sensory observations, or meaning as they are, while contextual meanings are the meanings of a lexeme or words that are in one context. (Chaer, 2012: 289-290). Meanings are everywhere, for example in literary works, scientific works, songs, etc. With the many types of meanings put forward by linguists

A lexical word or meaning is the meaning that corresponds to its referent, meaning that is in accordance with the results of observation of the senses, or meaning that is truly real in our lives, in other words, lexical meaning of a word is a real picture of a concept as the word symbolizes it (Chaer, 1990: 63).

Lexical meanings can also be considered as the meaning contained in a dictionary (Chaer, 1990: 63). Djajasudarma (1993: 34), expressing the lexical meaning is the meaning of the word that corresponds to what we encounter in the lexicon (dictionary). Lexical meanings can be searched in the dictionary. Chaer (2012: 289), describes lexical meaning as a meaning that is owned or existed in lexeme even without any context. The following will discuss some examples of words in sentences that have lexical meanings.

The phrase "the mouse got killed by the cat" contains the word mouse that has the lexical meaning of a rodent that can cause typhus. The word mouse in the sentence above refers to the animal mouse and not to others. We can see these mice in dirty places and usually roam inside the house, especially in hidden places. If you are not aware, these mice can damage foods and can cause disease when touched/eaten by humans.

Contextual meaning is a linguistic meaning in context. (Longman, 1992). For example, the meaning of a word is in a sentence or a sentence is in a paragraph. The sentence "do you know the meaning of war?" Has two different contextual meanings. The first contextual meaning in the question sentence, "do you know the meaning of the word war is?" The question sentence changes if expressed by a teacher to the students in the class. While the second contextual meaning is "war produces death, injury, and suffering", if expressed by a war-wounded soldier to politicians who support the war. 4 Kadmon (2001: 9), expressed his opinion about contextual meanings as follows: "Besides that, we talk about the" context of utterance.

"Each utterance occurs in a context. This context includes all sorts of things. It includes previous utterances. The speech situation, including location, speakers, addressees, various salient objects, and more. It includes various topics in the conversation, about the world in general and about the subject matter of the conversation in particular. It includes assumptions that interlocutors make about the beliefs and intentions of each other ". It can be concluded that in each phrase, there is a context.

The context in question varies, including the context of the situation, location, speaker, address, and other important objects. Context also includes various assumptions that participants have in the conversation. Chaer (2012: 290), expressing contextual meaning is the meaning of a lexeme or word that is in one context. The contextual meaning in the form of word-level can be seen from the following example. The sentence that says "You crocodile, he cheated his own mother!" has the contextual meaning of a rebellious child. The word "crocodile" in the sentence above refers to a child who willingly commits a crime of deception to his own parent without feeling guilty.

SEQUENCING OF SENTENCES & IMPROVING COMPREHENSION SKILLS

Sequencing "the identification of the components of a story- the beginning, middle, and end - and also to the ability to retell the events within a given text in the order in which they occurred". Sequencing is an essential strategy in comprehension, and the overall purpose of reading is comprehension.

Sequencing is one of many skills that contribute to students' ability to comprehend what they read. Sequencing refers to the identification of the components of a story — the beginning, middle, and end — and also to the ability to retell the events within a given text in the order in which they occurred.

Sequencing refers to putting events or information in a specific order. The ability to sequence requires higher-order thinking skills, from recognizing patterns to determining cause and effect, and more. Sequencing helps students understand and organize material they've learned as well as helps them solve problems.

There are 5 separate strategies that together form the high five reading strategy-

- Activating background knowledge. Research has shown that better comprehension occurs when students are engaged in activities that bridge their old knowledge with the new.
- Questioning.
- Analyzing text structure.

- Visualization.
- Summarizing.

Improve comprehension skills-

Comprehension strategies are conscious plans- sets of steps that good readers use to make sense of the text. Comprehension strategy instruction helps students become purposeful, active readers who are in control of their own reading comprehension. Certain steps that need to be followed to improve comprehension skills are:

- Eliminate distractions from your environment. The first step towards improving your reading comprehension has to be reading in a space where you'll be able to concentrate.
- Read with a helper if you're reading something above your level.
- Read aloud.
- Re-read text as necessary to improve your comprehension.

The "Super Six" comprehension strategies-
Such strategies are- Making Connections, Predicting, Questioning, Monitoring, Visualizing, and Summarizing.

1. **Making Connections-**

Students are encouraged to make personal connections from the text with: something in their own life, another text or something occurring in the world. Students focus on making connections in various activities via the Library and My Lessons. This occurs as students associate what they are reading, understanding and seeing with familiar situations and texts. For example, students predict what the book is about from an image of the front cover, using their skills in making connections. This can be followed up in classroom discussions by asking students to compare the books they read with other books and real-life situations. For example, asking children to 'explain to the class a time when you have experienced a similar feeling to a character in the book you read'. Or 'Does the front cover remind you of something you have experienced in your life?'

2. Predicting-

Students develop their predicting skills, using information from graphics, text and experiences to anticipate what will be read/ viewed/ heard and to actively adjust comprehension while reading/ viewing/ listening. In ABC Reading Eggs, prediction plays a significant part in introducing new texts to students, as they use cues from book covers, text and familiar words to make predictions about what the story is about. Students are encouraged to focuses on developing prediction skills throughout My Lessons and the Library, in the book notes and before reading activities. For example, in the My Lessons game "Arpiculate" students match each picture to its description. Students reveal sections of the picture tiles until they can predict what the whole picture is about. The faster and more accurately, students can answer, the more points they will earn.

3. Questioning-

Students learn to pose and answer questions that clarify meaning and promote a deeper understanding of the text. Books in the Library and My Lessons have quizzes at the start and/or the end of the book to encourage students to make predictions and draw conclusions from cues and also to test their level of understanding of the texts they read. Students are presented with a range of activities to develop their questioning skills including prediction, word understanding/meaning, dictionary meanings and word studies. For example, the "Audience and Purpose" questions in My Lessons help students as they answer questions to clarify the meaning of the text, encouraging students to develop a deeper understanding and a big picture view of text they read. The skills students develop online can be further consolidated at home or in the classroom by further questions from parents and teachers during a book reading to continue to support a child's understanding. Open-ended questions or questions that connect with a child's feelings toward the book can provoke further interest and engagement is often a great place to start.

4. Monitoring-

Students learn to stop and think about the text and know what to do when the meaning is disrupted. With all library books, students are given access to excerpts and can re-read texts at any point during the quiz so that they can be actively 'monitoring'. This ensures students have understood what they have read and encourages them to apply their knowledge in answering the questions to find deeper meanings.

5. Visualising-

Students create mental images from text they read/view/hear. Visualising brings the text to life, engages the imagination, and uses all of the senses. The books within ABC Reading Eggs have visual aids along with the text. However, the construction of the books use language that assists in developing a student's visualising skills as they learn to picture scenarios being presented to them in their heads. Quizzes also promote this recollection of images, where a student must draw on what they have read to answer questions that required visualizing. For example, the 'Picture this Sentence' quiz in the stadium, students are prompted to select the sentence that links most correctly to the picture displayed.

6. Summarising-

Students learn summarising skills as they identify and accumulate the most important ideas and restate them in their own words. This is also focused on in My Lessons and Library quizzes as many of the books have book notes and activities to encourage student understanding to be further drawn out. For example, 'Who, What, Where and When' and "Main Ideas and Details' questions in My Lessons and the end quizzes help students to identify and accumulate the most important ideas about the story as they make connections from what they have learnt.

Tips for helping struggling readers to improve reading comprehension-

- Find books they'll like.
- Read aloud.
- Skim the headings of the text.
- Re-read confusing sections.
- Use a ruler or finger to follow along.
- Write down words you don't know.

- Discuss what your child has just read.
- Recap and summarize the main points.
- Use different formats.
- Identify reading problems.
- Get a reading tutor.

<u>POINTS TO REMEMBER:</u>

- Consider where you read. Always read in a well-lit and quiet place that is free of distractions, and don't get into the habit of reading unit materials in bed! (unless you want to go to sleep).
- Don't vocalise as you read. This will slow you down, it won't help concentration, and it will lead to bad reading approaches.
- Read at times when you can concentrate, and maintain concentration by taking regular short breaks, perhaps every 30 or 45 minutes.
- Set yourself reading tasks (10 pages, 1 chapter, 1 section of a chapter, etc).
- Remember that reading often takes longer than you expect, and you often need to go beyond set texts. Give yourself enough time!

GLOSSARY:

- Topic Sentence- The topic sentence is the main point, or main idea of a paragraph. The topic sentence should identify the main idea and point of the paragraph.
- Types of Topic Sentences- General Topic Sentence, Clueing Topic Sentence and Specific Topic Sentence.
- Scanning- It is reading something rapidly for some specific piece of information. You can use this skill when you are in search of keywords.
- Skimming- It is a method of reading a text rapidly in order to get the basic overall idea.
- Previewing- Previewing means surveying a text quickly before you read it carefully. You preview when you want to get information.

CHAPTER FIVE

WRITING SKILLS

INTRODUCTION

In the modern era, the word 'Skill' is gaining a lot of attention because of its importance. A skill is an ability to do something in a well-developed manner and to make quick decisions. Skills can be categorized in types like job skills, personal skills, hard skills, soft skills, and many more. It got in use as per its requirement in various fields. Basic skills like listening, speaking, reading, and writing are necessary for achieving the goal. Strong skills can help to gain confidence and strong communication abilities. Knowledge and ability both are essential to hone the skills. Excellent writing skills are based on tact, tips and grammatical knowledge of it and ability to use correctly.

OBJECTIVES:

After successful completion of this chapter, you will be able to-

- Adopt writing skills.
- Understand the elements of writing skills and its types.
- Understand the role of diction in effective writing.
- Take steps for good writing.
- Understand paragraph and essay writing.
- Understand technical and literary writing.
- Identify common errors in writing.

WRITING AND WRITING SKILLS

When we talk about communication, traditionally two ways instantly click in our minds: oral and written. Written communication is more authentic and valuable to express one's views and ideas, as per its characteristics. Writing is the way of communication, by which one can impress through his/ her thoughts, whatever he wants to express to others.

The word 'Writing Skills' adds the word 'Skills' in writing, which means competence, expertise, and artistry. Writing is an art to express one's views, thoughts through words, but skill is a competence which enables the reader to understand the words exactly in the same sense as written by the writer.

Writing skills are such expertise abilities that present the ideas and information in a nicely written format for others to understand them. It organizes the knowledge and beliefs in a convincing manner. To put the feelings and opinions, writing skills help the writer to impress with voice, tone, mannerism, and body language without presenting himself/ herself in front of readers. Writing is a way of representing the ideas into textual forms to convey a message to the audience whereas writing skills have the ability to convert thoughts into words using proper grammar, punctuation, and essential well-structured aspects of writing.

Meaning and Definition of Writing Skills-

Harmer (2001:79) says that writing is a form of communication to deliver thought or to express feeling through written form. It means that writing is a productive skill that expresses feelings through written communication.

Jonah (2006:14) argues that writing is a series of activities going on and involves several phases, the preparatory phase, and the content development and review, as well as revisions or improvements posts.

According to **Gebhardt and Dawn Rodriguez** (19891) Writing is one of the most important things you do in school. Good writing skills take a big part to determine the success, whether it writing a report, proposal or assignment in school.

Peter T. Daniels (1996) defines "Writing as a system of more or less permanent marks used to represent an utterance in such a way that it can be recovered more or less exactly without the intervention of the utterer."

Lado (1971:272) says "Writing is a graphic representation of a language and information is conveyed through the written medium by the use of conventional graphemes."

Elbow (181:369) thinks of "Writing as a kind of 'magic' that can be performed by anyone who is involved in and believes in his tale". So, the process of translating abstract ideas into a concrete form is the art of writing."

Objectives of Writing Skill-

Writing skill includes the abilities to represent words using recorded signs. Here, we discuss some objectives of writing skills:

- To encompass intellectual or thinking skill.
- To encompass physical skills or the performance of actions.
- To present the attitude and values in written form.
- To target group/ audience for achieving the objectives of writing.
- To convey the message and opinion in front of the audience without the presence of the writer.
- Outline opportunities and offer effective strategies and activities for developing audience.
- Access the area of learning by writing skills.
- Apply effective techniques by writing skills to maximize performance.
- Understanding of the importance of good writing skills, basic rules of writing skills.
- Perfecting the language used in each of these new forms.
- Understanding of reading matter and in the application of grammatical forms.

Characteristics of Writing Skills-

In good writing, it is most essential that writing should have to be presented in such a manner, readers can conceive the message the same as written. These characteristics can be seen in effective writing:

- Clarity and Focus: Effective writing refines the thoughts and ideas into simple and easily considerable by the reader. No chance is left to be messed up with the complex sentences.

- Grammatically Strong: Effective writing has a strong matter with the use of correct grammar, punctuation, and rules of writing.
- Well Structured: A well-structured writing is not only clear but presented in a way that could be logical and easily understood to the audience.
- Efficient Vocabulary: This is the most important tool in writing. Good writing includes this element and uses accurate word choices and well-crafted sentences.
- Stimulation for Readers: Good writing affects edacious audiences. It inspires those readers to read fondly.
- Having Mental Notes: Special mental notes come from continuous observation and editing. It brings a special touch in writing.
- Well Editing and Re-evaluating: A good writer edits, again and again, rewrites and marks the improvements in his work to get better and effective writing.

TYPES OF WRITING SKILLS

Mainly four types of writing styles are seen, but some other types of styles are also here as under:

a. **Expository Writing:** This type of writing focuses on accepted facts. It does not include the author's views/ ideas and is totally based on the demand of the audience. In this style, the writer tries to explain those concepts which are accepted by a wider audience. Textbooks, recipes, news stories, business articles are some examples of expository writing.

b. **Descriptive writing:** This style describes a character, an event or a place in detail. The writer draws a picture as he likes, feels and notices. The author uses various adjectives, idioms and adverbs to makes the picture vivid for the readers. This style is used to write fictional stories/ novels/ poetry, journals, diary writing, and nature writing.

c. **Narrative writing:** Narrative writing is slightly different from descriptive writing. Unlike the descriptive writing, in this style author can create characters that carry a strong detail. It can be a fictional or non- fictional story. Writing stories requires a lot of imagination and effective writing skills to convey it to the readers. We can say, it uses creative writing on facts and figures, and not much attention is needed.

It frames dialogues, events, actions, emotions, novels, poetry (especially epic sages or poems), anecdotes, and oral histories are some examples that are written in this style.

d. **Persuasive writing:** As the word sounds, persuasive writing is written to persuade readers about what the author has written. It includes opinion justification, explanation, and personal point of view of the author. By his writing, he tries to convince the audience of a position or belief. In other words, we can say this style is "argumentative style", cover letters, editorial newspaper article, review of items, letter of recommendation come under this category. Generally, the writer's biasness with the thoughts and opinion is seen as evidence of the correctness of their position.

e. **Objective writing:** This is formal writing which uses facts and evidence. It statistically and scientifically proves the reason so that the reader could make his/her own opinion. In this style, the words like always, very and never are used.

f. **Creative writing:** As the name suggests, this writing is an art. This is not professional writing. It's aesthetic writing which is originated from author's imagination. Horror, crime, biographies, screens writing, script writing all come under this type of writing style.

g. **Review writing:** Review means analysis and to check or inspect any place, product, service or anything. The author writes his views/ experiences about books, product and soon. The best example of this is an online review about the product. It requires both persuasive as well as descriptive writing skills.

h. **Subjective writing:** This is an opinion-driven writing and follows the subjective approach. It is originated from the author's own experiences and observations. Basically, it is an insight feeling in the form of writing, which is the author's own unique perception.

IMPORTANCE OF GOOD WRITING SKILLS

A question arises why a skill is important for writing; skill is the most essential element to do any type of work. It enables a writer to communicate the message successfully with accuracy and correctness to the wider audience. Here are some benefits we will discuss which we get through good writing skills.

- **Easy Communication:** Communication is a medium to transfer the views, ideas, and opinions. It is very important for the development of a business as well as a country, without it we can't imagine to proceed with anything. Oral and written communications both have their own importance. Written communication makes a strong relation between receiver and sender. Good writing skills communicate word accuracy and efficiency that suits for development.

- **Important Profession:** Writing (written document) has its importance for official work. Skills in writing are the most essential to write a resume, business letter, reports, and much more. When someone is engaged to write, possessing outstanding writing abilities is necessary for the work.

- **Perceive as A Trustworthy and Credible Candidate:** By good writing skills, someone can prove her/himself as credible for the organization. It makes him dependable due to which he is assigned with more responsibility and considered as a right candidate for recruitment or for promotion.

- **Reflect the Persuasion:** Excellent convincing skills in writing inspire others to accomplish the goal. Skills bring innovation, and innovative ideas can enhance the motivation of the target and persuade them to accomplish the work efficiently.

- **Helps in Maintaining the Records:** To store some paperwork as a document, and record document that cannot be possible in oral communication, writing is a tool. Gathering information on paper is the genuine process of saving it for a long time.

- **Writing Skills Prove Strength of an Author:** The way of writing reflects the skill of an author. Grammar and punctuations are mentioned in effective writing correctly. It shows the capability of a writer and enhances the process of observation. Strong and excellent writing skills prove the author's intelligence and ability to fit for any job or for other tasks for which he is writing. He may be more influential than others only by way of writing.

- **Conveys Courtesy in Business:** In formal business, correspondence writing with skills covers the level of politeness and considerate attention to detail that is shown in face- to-face interaction. A courteous business letter expresses the writer's personal respect for the addressee, they work for.

- **Builds A Solid Web Presence:** Of late, online presentation is becoming popular. It helps potential customers discover the company and its products. Website, blogs and media accounts are maintained, but without efficient writing skills, there are not effective.

SENTENCE FORMATION

What is a Sentence? A group of words giving a meaningful sense is called a sentence. It must contain a subject and a verb followed by a part of speech. A single word cannot complete a meaning. For making a sentences author uses many grammatical rules. Correct sentence formation makes an author's writing justified. Parts of speech provide a framework to write any idea clearly and effectively.

Definition of sentence formation- "The grammatical arrangement of words in sentences is called a sentence structure."

"A sentence is a collection of words that convey sense or meaning and is formed according to the logic of grammar."

"A sentence is a set of words that is complete in itself, typically containing a subject and predicate, conveying a statement, question, exclamation, or command, and consisting of a main clause and sometimes one or more subordinate clauses."

Elements of a Sentence-

- A sentence provides a clear meaning to the author's written matter.
- It follows the rules of grammar.
- Correct punctuation is necessary to explain complete sense.
- Two or more noun, pronoun and verb may be used according to the types of sentence.
- It draws the framework for writing to an author.
- A sentence can be in the form of a question, a statement, an exclamation or command.

Types of Sentences-

Basically, sentences are of four types, but some other types of sentences also can be seen. We will explain all these with examples ahead. So that it could be easily understood.

1. Simple and Declarative sentence

This is a simple statement which states a fact and ends with a full stop (period). It contains one independent clause. For example-
(i) Ramesh goes to the cinema hall to watch a movie.
(ii) He is an intelligent boy.

2. Compound sentence

When two or more simple sentences are written jointly, it is called a compound sentence. These sentences have an independent clause that may or may not be connected with conjunction like and, so, but, yet, because and so on. It can also be joint with a comma or semi-colon. For example- (i) Chirag likes to read comics; he feels fresh after that. (ii) John has an antique watch because he is fond of collecting antiques.

3. Complex sentence

These types of sentences combine both dependent and independent clauses. A complex sentence can start by any clause either dependent or independent clause, but if it begins with a dependent clause, it is separated from the independent clause with the 'comma' simply. But, if independent clause comes first, the words like although, as, even though, if, instead, when, whenever, where, while are used to joint dependent clause. For example- (i) If you work hard, you will definitely get success. (ii) I want to reach there where you want to go. (ii) Although he earns well, he is still unhappy with his job.

4. Compound-Complex Sentence

As the rule of complex sentences, it begins with a dependent clause separated from the central clause by a comma. In compound-complex sentences, the rule for both types of compound and complex sentences is followed. Dependent and independent, both clauses are used. At the end of the sentence, the independent clause is joined by a comma and the word or, as in the rule for the compound. So, a compound complex sentence is made up of more than one sentence joined by a conjunction, and at least one of those sentences is complex. For example- (i) I will go to the market, but first, I have to complete my homework after I prepare the tea. (ii) When I woke up in the morning, I saw the birds' chirping in the garden, and it made me happy.

5. Imperative Sentence

This sentence shows command, order, or request. It ends with a mark of a period (full stop). For example- (i) Open the door. (ii) Please give me a glass of water.

6. Interrogative Sentence

This type of sentence is used for asking something, and this ends with question mark (?). For example- (i) Where are you going? (ii) May I borrow your shirt for some days?

7. Exclamatory Sentence

It is used for showing exclamations like emotion, grief, happiness etc. It ends with an exclamation mark (!). For showing exclamatory expressions like wow, alas, hurray, oho, bravo, fantastic ouch, etc is used before exclamation sign. As- (i) Wow! It's amazing. (ii) Hurray! We won. (iii) Oh! I forgot my notebook at my home.

<u>Tips to Be Kept in Mind in Sentence Formation/ Structure-</u>

A good sentence structure helps to eliminate the use of sentence fragments as well. A sentence fragment is an incomplete sentence. So, under mentioned are some tips to be kept in mind while forming a sentence:

- Be careful not to err on the side of a run-on sentence to avoid a sentence fragment. A run-on sentence is when two or more independent clauses are joined without appropriate punctuation or conjunction.
- Get the words in the right order. The most common order for the part of the sentence is subject, verb, and object.

- Be aware of punctuation that can present a sentence correctly. One may decide whether to use a comma with the subordinate clause in a complex sentence.
- Do not use "you" or "myself" in the imperative sentence.
- Do not use a question mark in a declarative sentence but the interrogative sentence must end with a question mark.
- Check carefully for the subject and verb in the text after conjunction to confirm the text is an independent clause.

DICTION

Sentence formation and use of proper diction both are important in writing and come under writing skills of an author. Diction has its own place in writing. It is an accent, inflexion, intonation and speech-sound quality manifested by an individual speaker or writer. It separates good from bad writing. Proper diction is important to get the message across. According to an article, proper diction in writing follows three rules-

- Choice of the accurate and right word.
- Choice of the appropriate word according to context.
- Choice of reader's/ listener's understandable words easily.

<u>Definitions of diction-</u>

Diction can be defined as 'style of speaking or writing, determined by choice of words by a speaker or a writer'.

Diction (Latin: dictionem (nom. dictio), "a saying, expression, word"

According to dictionary.com (Thesaurus.com), "Diction is a style of speaking or writing as dependent upon the choice of words."

Aristotle, in the Poetics (20) states that, "Diction comprises of eight elements: Phoneme, Syllable, Conjunction, Connective, Noun, Verb, Inflection and Utterance."

In simple words, "Diction is the choice, and use of words in speech or writing" or "Diction is the way and manner in which somebody pronounces different words".

NOTE- Reasons behind to learn diction.

- To create correct phraseology and phrasing.

- To establish a narrative voice and tone.
- To establish the support to setting for the story.
- To pursue readers and entertain them with the correct choice of words.

Types of Diction-

Diction depends on the occasion and on the type of audiences. It reflects the character's detail like age, background, profession etc. Types of diction depict the way of expressing different ideas. Types of Diction are as follows:

- **Formal Diction**

In formal diction, the language used is formal. This language contains polite and proper words that are descriptive. Conference Presentation, Business document, and legal papers are all prepared in formal language. Generally, formal diction is used in formal situations.

- **Informal Diction**

It is conversational and narrative language which is used in informal situations like talking to friends, personal mail, and letters, etc. Informal language is the relaxed language that we use in our daily life routine.

- **Neutral/ standard Diction**

It refers to the level of diction employed, writing assignment at college level and newspaper. It maintains a professional tone but tries to avoid highly technical or specialized term as formal diction.

- **Colloquial Diction**

It refers to non- standard languages like regional. It is also known as an appropriate language to informal or conversational language and speech of writing. Example: anyhow, gotcha, stats, info, guys, etc.

- **Abstract Diction**

The term abstract refers to ideas or concepts which are untouched by the writer. The writer uses words to express something intangible. The author does not experience this through his five senses.

- **Concrete Diction**

It is opposite of abstract diction. It uses those words which have a literal meaning and relate to things that appeal to the senses.

- **Poetic Diction**

It consists of lyrical words that relate to a poem creating a euphonious or harmonious sound.

Importance of Diction-

1. Diction conveys the author's attitude, tone towards the topic.
2. It impacts on argument as well as the author's credibility.
3. Show the strength of writing by ensuring the full range of meaning of the words that the writer has used.
4. Appropriate everywhere, whether academic writing, professional writing or business writing.
5. The writer's tone can influence the reader's response towards the writing.

PARAGRAPH AND ESSAY WRITING

Paragraph writing-

Genres of writing are known as types of writing. Literary genres and professional genres both have their own importance. From a small sentence to an essay, writing comes across a number of elements and covers a number of styles. According to the syllabus, we will discuss paragraph writing, essay writing, technical writing, and literary writing one by one.

Meaning-

A paragraph is a group of sentences by which the author keeps his ideas (central) and tries to brainstorm logics behind the writing. A well-structured paragraph can be the backbone of any literature. Length of literature decides a number of paragraphs and the length of a paragraph depends on the information it conveys. A paragraph has a sequential series of sentences. This is because the reader could know the organization of thoughts in an essay or any literature (writing) and subdivided to define the beginning and end. It might describe a place, character or process; it may narrate or compare a series of events.

Definition of paragraph writing-

According to Lunsford and Connors, "A paragraph is defined as "a group of sentences or a single sentence that forms a unit"

"A paragraph is a subdivision of a written composition that consists of one or more sentences, deals with one point or gives the words of one speaker, and begins on a new usually indented line. "Or it can be defined as "Paragraph has sequential series of a sentence".

Paragraph Structure-

Describing, comparing, contrasting or controlling information can all be used to structure a paragraph by following these points:

- **Topic Sentence:** Topic sentence is a focus sentence. It organizes the entire paragraph. This topic sentence summarizes the main idea of a paragraph.
- **Supporting Idea:** This supports the main idea, means, it is more focused on arguments that strengthen the main ideas.
- **Adding Detail:** To bolster the paragraph writing, add a few sentences. These sentences describe the details of the further storyline.
- **Concluding Sentence:** This concluding sentence in a paragraph brings closure to the main idea. This is a final thought about the topic on which they are writing. Generally, this sentence starts with: therefore, overall, thus, finally, lastly, for this reason, and so on.

Characteristics of paragraph writing-

In writing, paragraph formation is most essential. A small paragraph presents the whole picture of the objective for writing. A good paragraph has these characteristics:

- **Unity:** The whole paragraph represents a single sense or thought. As the paragraph is made by group of sentences that depends on each other.
- **Order:** In a paragraph, sentences are organized in a sequence. That's why a paragraph contains a series of sentences. This series connects each other to present the main idea effectively. So, it follows the specific step by step order.
- **Content Length:** No one likes to read a long paragraph because it deviates the reader's mind and makes it boring. It concludes that a good paragraph is the one that have a proper length of content.
- **Coherence:** Paragraph presents the sentences in coherence. All sentences of a paragraph should relate to each other.
- **Binding:** This is the main characteristics of paragraph writing. It bounds a reader to read. The reader feels interesting to continue reading.

Steps to Write a Paragraph-

To construct a fine paragraph, a writer should follow these steps:

- Decide the topic of your paragraph
- Develop a topic sentence
- Demonstrate your point
- Give your paragraph meaning
- Conclude
- Look over and proofreading

Essay Writing:

The word 'essay' is derived from Latin word "exagium" which means 'presenting a case' and from French word 'essayer' which means "to try" or "to attempt". An essay has everything that needs to be said. An essay contains a selection of topic, critical evaluation, organization, and presentation of facts. It is considered synonymous with a story or a paper or an article covering the serious topics. An essay can be formal as well as informal.

Definition of an essay-

A famous English essayist, Aldous Huxley defines essays as "A literary device for saying almost everything and anything". According to Oxford Dictionary, 'Essay is a short piece of writing on a particular subject."

Characteristics of good essay writing-

- **Well Developed**-An essay has a series of paragraphs. All paragraphs connect with each other to come out at the end and describe the story in short. All it is well developed by an essayist.
- **Discipline**- Essay is not too short as a paragraph. It makes a chain of thoughts and keeps a picture before the audience as a short story. It is descriptive in nature.
- **Unambiguous**-Essay is written to the point and focus on any serious topic or any event. It should be written univocal, always maintaining the main content of the essay.
- **Subjected**- Good essay writing consist subjectivity with the topic. An essayist always maintains a great intonation till the completion of essay.
- **Argumentation**- If the author wants to make an essay reading interesting and binds the reader; he tries to put arguments and disagreements in the essay. So, a good essay must be argumentative.
- **Anecdotal**- An essay covers a story or an event or a serious topic. It can be biographical, incidental, accidental, or historical. To narrate any of them may be helpful to the society. An essay is aimed to show writers personal opinion about the subject.
- **Organized**-An excellent essay organizes all paragraphs in such a way that conveys full information to the readers. It represents an order to structure an essay.

Types of Essay Writing-

a. **Definition Essay:** The point of this type of essay is to explain something on a higher level than dictionaries do. Definition essay aims to define the subject in a few sentences.

b. **Compare and Contrast Essay:** An essay can be written upon on differences and similarities between objects or event. This type of essay is known as a compare and contrast essay.

c. **Cause and Effect Essay:** Essay reminds a study where essayist writes to show what cause has led to a particular result. This type of essay shows the logical connection between cause and effect.

d. **Process Essay:** Basically, this type of writing is used to write a paper. It requires the same level of understanding of the subject, and it works.

e. **Argumentative Essay:** This type of essay writing aims to change the reader's attitude towards something. It is written to manipulate people's thoughts to create their interest.

f. **Critical Essay:** This critical essay presents the writer's thought analytically. It defines 'Good' and 'Bad' consideration of the problem. The purpose of writing this type of essay is to focus on weak and strong features of something (problem).

g. **Expository Essay:** Writer's own experience is presented in an expository essay. It requires a lot of knowledge about the subject. Expository essays are the exposition of the writer's knowledge and research.

h. **Persuasive Essay:** The topic of this type of essay is related that are relevant here and today. Persuasive essays are very tough and influential. These essays require a better understanding of the subject and goodwill.

i. **Descriptive Essay:** A descriptive essay describes a place, an object, an event in depth. One clever way to do that is to evoke the senses of the reader.

j. **Narrative essay:** It is like storytelling, about a certain event in personal life. Events, for example: watching cinema, festival celebration, etc are written in this form. Usually, it is written in the first person.

<u>Tips for Writing an Excellent Essay-</u>

- Keep the word limit of an essay short. It should not be too long for the reader to feel bored. The limit should be between 300-500 words.
- An essay must be traversed around the central idea giving an appropriate and interesting title so that the readers can create interest to read it.
- Keep the language simple and crisp.
- It must be free from grammatical errors.

- Before starting to write an essay, the writer should re-look into the thought and organize it in a sequential manner.
- Proofread again and check the errors.
- End the essay with completing a subject.

Steps to be taken while writing an essay-

- Develop a topic.
- Taking critical notes and read carefully by conducting research
- Create a research statement
- Integrated research evidence is used in formally formatting the essay
- At last, edit, view, and revise.

TECHNICAL AND LITERARY WRITING

Technical Writing-

In the 20th century, technical writing had its place and was officially recognized. Technical writing was in high demand and became an official job title during World War II. Complex writing machines were being invented. Universities, library, engineering, military hardware, aerospace led to technical writing. With the growing popularity of computers the field of technical writing also grew.

Technical writing is significantly different from other types of writing, like narrative, because technical writing is intended to impart some specific skill or ability. This style of writing has a very different purpose and different characteristics according to the purpose than other writing styles such as creative writing. Technical writing is done to educate, informing, or directing someone on how to do something.

Technical writing required strong technical skill. It also requires a writer to examine the audience extensively.

Definition of technical writing-

The traditional definition of technical writing is: "Technical writing is the practice of documenting processes, such as software manuals or instructional materials. Traditionally, it was limited to user manuals of some sort."

Today technical writing encompasses all documentation of complex technical processes. It includes reports, executive summary statements and briefs. Each time technical information is conveyed in writing at work, it is, by definition, technical writing.

Characteristics of Technical writing-

- It is straight forward and clear.
- Use of computer is important for technical documentation.
- Technical writing is done for a specialized topic.
- Providing instructions about how to do a particular task.
- Technical writing covers a wide range of genres and technologies like press release, memo, reports, etc.
- Need for awareness about the audience's existing knowledge.
- Technical writing takes much more time to write.
- Technical writing is detailed and informative.
- Technical writing is done in a concise and well-structured manner.

Genres of Technical writing-

This type of writing covers different styles depending on the audience and information. These styles include proposals, procedures and instructions, press release, e-mail, letters memoranda, resume, job application, case study, etc.

Tips for good Technical Writing-

If a writer keeps in mind the following tips, he can easily and quickly explain any complex piece of writing:

- Know about your audience for whom writing is done because in technical writing, a complex language is used and many abbreviations, acronyms are directly applied to such a field according to the audience.
- Use an impersonal style.
- A writer must write in simple and straight forward language which a reader can understand easily.
- Collection of information must be analysed thoroughly.
- Information must be arranged into an understandable and conceivable format.

- Check repeatedly after writing. It should not be lengthy and monotonous for the reader.

<u>Skills needed for Technical Writing-</u>

A successful technical writing has to have set of skills like good written communication skill, document design skill, fluency with digital tools, graphic software knowledge, screen capture tool, web developing tools, component management systems, and desktop publishing tools or word process, abbreviations, acronyms and technical language that make a technical writing efficient.

Literary writing

Literary writing is creative writing and used in fiction. For this writing, personal motivation of a writer is essential. It is an art and a depiction of thoughts and views in writing as poem, story, novel and any form of literature. Literature word is derived from the Latin word meaning "writing formed with letters." Literature is a form of human expression which is organized and written down in expressive manner. Literature also functions more broadly in society as a means of both criticizing and affirming cultural values.

<u>Definition of literary writing-</u>

Definition of the word literature tends to be circular. The 11th edition of Merriam-Webster's Collegiate Dictionary considers literature to be "Writing having excellence of form or expression and expressing ideas of permanent or universal interest."

The 19th-century critic Walter Pater referred to "The matter of imaginative or artistic literature" as a transcript, not of mere fact, but of fact in its infinitely varied forms."

According to thesaurus.com, "Literature is writing in which expression and form, in connection with ideas of permanent and universal interest, are characteristics or essential features, as poetry, novels, history, biography, and essays."

Features of Literary Writing-

- It has a narrative element.
- Literary writing is the reflection of ideas, passions of human being.
- It is an art, having creativity.
- It paints a picture of author's feelings like a real world.
- Objective of literary writing is to provide information to the audience.
- It is done as an intellectual and imaginative work.

Functions of literary writing-

- **Knowledge Sharing:** Through literature, the writer shares the knowledge, information, thoughts, and ideas with audience creatively.
- **Entertainment:** Literary writing gets the wonder feel to the audience. The writer presents his idea in an influence manner. **Shaping the Aesthetic Sense:** Literature describes behaviour, attitude and all in an aesthetic sense. It helps us to notice everything beautiful around us.
- **Self- Development:** Through literature, an author helps himself with new ideas and information. Readers inhale all those qualities and knowledge what he reads in books and magazines.
- **Transformation:** A good literature can transform a reader's behaviour, attitude and bad memories into good and beautiful. The audience get inspired with it.

Genres of literary writing-

The styles of literary writing include the way to write literature or can be said in other words 'style' in which it is performed. Normally, these genres are familiar: Poetry, Prose, Drama, essay, fable, and fiction and non-fiction are often divided into sub-genres.

<u>Steps to be Taken While Writing a Literature</u>

- To understand the purpose of literary writing.
- To decide the format.
- Execute the plan of how to write and what you analyse to write.
- Now start writing.
- After completion of literary writing, edit your work.

COMMON ERRORS IN WRITING:

Without using grammar in a sentence, it can't make complete sense. Grammar exposes the author's thought and ideas in the same manner as those are. A minor error distracts readers from understanding the author's writing. So, it's very important to be alert about the errors and keep all those in mind. Here we discussed some errors which commonly occur unknowingly or due to negligence of knowledge about grammar:

Without using grammar in a sentence, it can't make complete sense. Grammar exposes the author's thought and ideas in the same manner as those are. A minor error distracts readers from understanding the author's writing. So, it's very important to be alert about the errors and keep all those in mind. Here we discussed some errors which commonly occur unknowingly or due to negligence of knowledge about grammar:

1. Errors about Singular- Plural related to Subject-Verb

The verb of a sentence must be according to the subject. If the subject of the sentence is singular, its verb must also be singular; and if the subject is plural, the verb must also be plural. Example:

Incorrect: An essential chapter of that book has been missing. Correct: An essential chapter of that book has been missing.

2. Incompleteness of Sentence

Incomplete sentence due to number of clauses is called a sentence fragment. A fragment may lack a subject, a complete verb, or both. Sometimes fragments depend on the proceeding sentence to give it meaning. **Example:**

Incorrect: He gave a treat to all his friends. Despite of the fight. Correct: Despite of the fight, he gave a treat to all his friends.

3. Errors related to use of a comma

'Comma' is used in many senses to give a proper meaning to a sentence. Due to misuse of it, meaning can differ. Here, some errors are discussed which are usually occurred with the misuse of 'comma' like:

- **Missing comma:** A comma should be used after an introductory word, phrase, or clause. This gives the reader a slight pause after an introductory element and often can help avoid confusion. Example:

Incorrect: Before she could stop him the kid rang their neighbor's bell.
Correct: Before she could stop him, the kid rang their neighbor's bell.

- **Comma with a conjunction:** A comma separates two or more independent clauses in a compound sentence separated by a conjunction. The comma goes after the first clause and before the coordinating conjunction that separates the clauses. Example:

Incorrect: He was handsome and he was successful and he was full of life. Correct: He was handsome, successful, and full of life.

- **Superfluous Commas:** To throw commas around liberally when they aren't necessary is occurred. Example:

Incorrect: The woman never sang in public, because she was not comfortable to sing in front of a crowd.
Correct: The woman never sang in public because she was not comfortable to sing in front of a crowd.

- **Splice of a comma:** A comma splice occurs when two separate sentences are joined with a comma rather than a period or semicolon. Writers often create comma splices when using transitional words, such as however, therefore, moreover, nevertheless, or furthermore. Example:

Incorrect: My plan was to go out for a movie, however I had to cancel that due to an urgent meeting.
Correct: My plan was to go out for a movie; however, I had to cancel that due to an urgent meeting.

4. Misplaced or Dangling Modifier

A misplaced modifier is a word, phrase, or clause that is improperly separated from the word it modifies or describes. Sentences with this error can sound awkward, ridiculous, or confusing. A dangling modifier is a word or phrase that modifies a word not clearly stated in the sentence. **Example:**
Incorrect: While walking along the beach, Silvia found a sparkly girl's set of earring. Correct: While walking along the beach, Silvia found a girl's sparkly set of earring.

5. Wrong Word Usage

There are a variety of words and phrases that are commonly confused and misused in sentences. So before using homophones, the word having the same pronunciation but different meaning, the author must go through its meaning carefully. There are hundreds of these commonly confused words; here we will see the difference in the use of similar pronunciation word because of their spelling. Example:

Incorrect: I never want to loose a good friend like Sita.

Correct: I never want to lose a good friend like Sita.

For examples, some other words that create confusion are:

- To/ too/two
- There/ their
- Lose/loose
- Mare/ mere
- Buy/by
- Hole/whole
- Write/right
- Week/weak
- Steal/steel and many more.

6. Lounge Sentence

A sentence can become a burden to read when there are too many equally weighted phrases. These make it lengthy and boring for readers. Example:

Incorrect: Jason was planning to attend his friend's wedding on June 30, but at the last minute he found out he had a jury duty, so he couldn't attend the wedding, and he felt really guilty about it.

Correct: Unexpectedly, Jason was called for jury duty and couldn't attend his friend's June 30 wedding. He felt guilty about missing it.

7. Colon Mistakes

A colon is used after a complete sentence to introduce a word, phrase, clause, list, or quotation. The colon signals that what follows proves or explains the sentence preceding the colon. Example:

Incorrect: People move to cities for: the better lifestyle, high paying jobs, and a good atmosphere.

Correct: People move to cities for three reasons: better lifestyle, high paying jobs and good atmosphere.

8. Errors in Using Infinitive

An infinitive is the word "to" with a verb. There are no grammar rules that prohibit split infinitives, but many experts disapprove of them. If the sentence sounds awkward by correcting the split, our rule of thumb is to go with, what makes the most sense in the context of your writing and for the ease of reading. Example:

Incorrect: She tried to quickly finish her breakfast before she had to leave. Correct: She tried to finish the breakfast quickly before she had to leave.

9. Errors in using Apostrophes

The apostrophe is used for a purpose, either to indicate a possession (implying ownership) or a contraction (in place of other letters). Since, its use to indicate a contraction is easiest, we will deal with this first. But, if it is used wrongly, the meaning of a sentence can be misunderstood by the readers or it might sound awkward. It can be explained by the following examples:

   a. Using Apostrophes to Indicate Contraction- Where one or more letters have been dropped, an apostrophe is used as a replacement:

- It is = it's
- We are = we're
- Does not = Doesn't
- Of the clock = o'clock Example:

Incorrect: I don't believe its finally Friday. Correct: I don't believe it's (it is) finally Friday.

   b. Using Apostrophes to Indicate Possession- Apostrophes are also used to indicate possession/ custody or occupancy. Matthew's car

- The teachers' staff room
- The farmers' fields (multiple fields owned by multiple farmers)

   c. When Not to Use Apostrophes- If the word is a plural, then do not use an apostrophe like people, children. There are possible exceptions to this rule are if the word comprises a single letter, a number or abbreviation where the simple addition of an s could cause confusion. Hence:

There are three r's in word 'Error'.

To write "There are three rs in word 'Error' may confuse the reader even though it is grammatically correct. Alternatively, you could rephrase this as "There are three "r"s in the word 'Error'.

10. Unnecessary or Missing Capitalization

Use capitalization with a proper noun, pronoun, adjective, first words of sentences, and highlights of important words in titles. Example:

Incorrect: there are many ways to skin a cat. Correct: There are many ways to skin a cat.

11. Unnecessary Hyphen

The use of hyphens has combined all of these words into a single word. Hyphen is used between parts of a compound name or words. It serves to remove confusion from sentences and to combine multiple words to form a single meaning. Example:

Generation-Z is tech-savvy.

I want to buy blue-coloured shirt.

Using hyphen, a writer must keep in mind these characteristics:

- If a compound adjective comes before the noun, they are hyphenated.
- If a compound adjective comes after the noun, there is no hyphen.
- The hyphen is omitted with such compound adjectives as well as adjectives preceded by adverbs that end in '-ly' such as:

Writing being a complicated task, language might be confusing due to its spelling and grammar checkers that will not differentiate between some of the often-used words that are confusing.

POINTS TO REMEMBER:

- The word 'Writing Skills' adds the word 'Skills' in writing, which means competence, expertise, and artistry. Writing is an art to express views and thoughts through words, but skill is a competence which enables to understand the words exactly in the same sense as the writer has written.
- Clarity and Focus, Grammatically Strong, Well Structured, Efficient Vocabulary, Stimulation for Readers, Having Mental Notes, Well Editing and Re-evaluating are the essential characteristics which makes good writing.

- Mainly four types of writing are seen: Expository Writing, Descriptive writing, Persuasive writing and Narrative writing. Also, some other sub-styles are used in writing like Objective writing, Subjective writing, Creative writing, Review writing, etc.

- Skill is the most essential element for any type of task. It enables a writer to communicate the message successfully with accuracy and correctness to the wider audience. It makes him dependable, assigned with more responsibility and makes him the right candidate for recruitment as well as promotion. Also, helps in maintaining the Records.

- The grammatical arrangement of words in sentences is called sentence formation." An effective sentence has to involve the clear meaning, rules of grammar, correct punctuation etc. all these elements in his writing. We use a different type of sentence in writing like Simple and Declarative sentence, Compound sentence, Complex sentence, Compound- complex sentence, Command and imperative sentence, Question and Interrogative sentence, Exclamatory sentence.

- Diction is an accent, inflexion, intonation, and speech sound quality manifested by an individual speaker or writer. It separates good from bad writing. Diction is of many types: Formal Diction, Informal Diction, Neutral/ standard Diction, Colloquial Diction, Abstract Diction, Concrete Diction, Poetic Diction. Diction conveys the author's attitude, a tone, which can influence the reader's response to the writing towards the topic. It shows the strength of writing and the author's credibility by ensuring the full range of meaning of the words that the writer uses.

- A paragraph has a sequential series of sentences. This is because the reader could know the organization of thoughts in an essay or any literature (writing) and subdivided to define begins and end. For structuring a paragraph, a writer has to follow four component topic sentences, supporting ideas, adding detail, concluding sentence step by step. A paragraph contains unity, order, content length and coherence.

- The word 'essay' is derived from Latin word "exagium" which means 'presenting a case' and in French, word 'essayer' which means "to try" or "to attempt". A famous English essayist, Aldous Huxley defines essays as, 'a literary device for saying almost everything about almost anything" An essay must be well disciplined, unambiguous, argumentative, anecdotal and well organized. It is written in many different forms like definition Essay, compare and contrast essay, cause and effect essay, process essay, critical essay, expository essay, persuasive essay, narrative essay, and many more. When essayist starts to write an essay, he should follow some steps keeping in mind the word limit and give an appropriate and interesting title so that readers can create interest to read it. Language should be simple and crisp, free from grammatical errors and sequentially organized.

- The main difference between a paragraph and an essay is that a paragraph is composed of three-four sentences ending with a concluding sentence while essay has multiple paragraphs and ends with a conclusion paragraph.

- Traditionally, two types of writing are seen: technical writing and literary writing. Technical writing is done for the purpose of educating, informing or directing someone on how to do something. A computer is used to write this type of writing; it is straight forward and clear. Technical writing is written in a concise and well-structured manner. Proposal, document, business letter, etc use this technical writing. A specific skill is needed in technical writing.

- Literary writing is creative writing and used in fiction. It is an art and a depiction of thoughts and views as poem, story, novel and any form of literature. Literature is a word derived from the Latin word meaning "writing formed with letters. Literature is a form of human expression which is organized and written down in an expressive manner. It serves society in terms of knowledge sharing, entertainment, shaping the aesthetic sense, self- development and transformation of society.

- Sometimes, a writer gets stuck in his writing due to occurrence of some errors. Incompleteness of Sentence, errors related to use of comma, dangling modifier, wrong word usage, lounge Sentence, colon mistakes, errors in using infinitive, errors in using apostrophes, incorrect word, and capitalization are some common errors that must be acknowledged by an author. Error correction is very important to keep the audience engaged to your piece of writing.

GLOSSARY:

- **Expository Writing-** A type of writing focusing on accepted facts.
- **Descriptive writing-** This style of writing describes a character, an event or a place in detail.
- **Narrative writing-** Narrative writing is a style where the author can create characters that carry a strong detail.

- **Persuasive writing**- As the word sounds, persuasive writing is written to persuade the readers about what the author has written.
- **Objective writing**- This is formal writing which uses facts and evidence. It statistically and scientifically proves the reason so that the reader could make own opinion.
- **Creative writing**- As the name suggests, this writing is an art. It's aesthetic writing which is originated from author's imagination. Horror, crime, biographies, screens writing, script writing all come under this type of writing style.
- **Review writing**- Review means analysis and to check or inspect any place, product, service or anything. The author writes his views/ experiences about books, product and soon. The best example of this is online review about the product.
- **Subjective writing**- This is an opinion driven writing and follows subjective approach. It is originated from an author's own experiences and observations. Basically, it is an insight feeling in the form of writing that is the author's own unique perception.

CHAPTER SIX

PROPOSALS

INTRODUCTION

No proposal can be drafted at all without skills and knowledge. It is important to know how to use both of these. However, both seem to be same actually, they are not. By knowledge, can understand the concept and help give the track but skill gives shape to particular thing filled with feelings.

So, skill is an application and practical approach. For writing a successful proposal, communication skill with good writing is most essential. A good proposal may be helpful to communicate full information to their customers.

In economic world, a proposal has an important place. Whether a company or an organization wants to build good connections with customers and wants to increase the sale, or customers want to get a product which meets their requirements, everywhere there is a need to write a good proposal. A good proposal attracts and fulfils all the needs of that person who writes the proposal with any purpose.

OBJECTIVES

After successful completion of this chapter, you will be able to-

- Understand proposal types and their components.
- Know the features of a proposal.
- Draft business proposals.
- Draft project proposals.

WHAT IS A PROPOSAL?

In the business world, proposal is an important document that ploughs the initial relationship between organizations and customers. The proposal frames the extensive information in such a way that can achieve the goal to write this proposal. It is helpful to eliminate the stones by including the information. A proposal is used by the sales person to meet the specific needs required by the customers. It seems like an estimation but estimation and proposal both are different documents. For small businesses, it may be the same. Nevertheless, it is vital to remember that proposals are always first and foremost sales document. It is an offer to finally manage to get what you want in an argument or business agreement.

Definition-

- According to the British English dictionary "A proposal is a plan or an idea, often a formal or written one, which is suggested for people to think about and decide upon."
- Wallace and Van Fleet say that "A proposal is a form of persuasive writing; every element of every proposal should be structured and tailored to maximize its persuasive impact."

In a nutshell, a proposal is a document that is prepared for a prospective customer to persuade the prospect to adopt the solution to a problem or the fulfilment of a need proffered in the proposal. Proposals are written for both private and public sector organizations."

<u>Characteristics of a proposal-</u>

- A proposal is an informative document.
- A proposal may be used as a report.
- A proposal is written in a structured form.
- It impacts persuasive writing.
- It identifies the strategy of an organization.
- It is helpful to outline the plan/ research design.

<u>Proposal and Proposal Writing-</u>

a. A proposal is a document whereas writing proposal is a process.

b. A proposal contains all important information about organization whereas writing a proposal is a thinking and persuasive process.

c. Proposals are of many types whereas writing proposal contains many steps.

d. A proposal is an already prepared form (or a complete document) whereas proposal writing needs skill requirement to shape a proposal.

TYPES OF PROPOSAL

There are many types of proposals. These can be categorized according to the particular aim of the person who writes the proposal. It may be academic, professional, and commercial. Here, in a simple manner, it is categorized into four types- Internal Proposal, External Proposal, Solicited Proposal, and Unsolicited Proposal.

1. Internal Proposal-

A proposal that is written within the same organization, department may vary, is called an internal proposal. It is not too lengthy and is not required to explain much in detail. We can say it is not very explanatory.

2. External Proposal-

A proposal which is written to a certain organization/ government/ business, including a lot of information is called an external proposal. It is written for some specific purpose.

3. Solicited Proposal-

A proposal which is based on request for a proposal to be sent, by the recipient / customer is called solicited proposal. They may ask verbally, or they may issue a written request for the proposal. This proposal has a specific purpose.

4. Unsolicited Proposal-

This type of proposal does not have specific requirements. However, it is most valuable for starting to write the proposal. It is in the form of a casual conversation.

Types of Business Proposals-

A business proposal is a document written in a business-related context. These are used to make a plan or design the path for increasing sale and increasing marketing of the products or services, etc. These can also be divided into three types- Formally Solicited Business Proposal, Informally Solicited Business Proposal, and Unsolicited Solicited Business Proposal.

1. <u>Formally Solicited Business Proposal</u>

To meet the business requirements, Formally Solicited Business Proposals are created by the company for their recipients like customers or an audience. Formally Solicited Business Proposal is prepared in such a structure with the aim to quantify the needs of the business. The following types of Formally Solicited Business Proposal are used in an organization:

a. **Request for Quotation (RFQ):** Quotation is a document which contains the information like time period, cost specific, terms of services, etc. A customer issues the proposal to the supplier when there is a need of large quantity of goods.
b. **Request for Proposal (RFP):** Basically, it is written by the customer's side in order to meet their needs regarding product or services if available product or service is not up to their satisfaction level or what they want.
c. **Invitation for Bid (IFB):** Bid is an offer or an effort to do something and to pay a particular price for the same. It is done to check the price, when a customer wants to get the required services, then IFBs are issued.
d. **Request for Information (RFI):** This is the first proposal above all. The purpose of writing the RFI is to get information about the product, services, vendors etc. It gives the shape to further decision.

2. <u>Informally Solicited Business Proposal</u>

Informally Solicited Business Proposal is the descriptions of the vendor, product or prospective customer based on a conversation with key issues. They do not contain formal requirements to respond.

3. <u>Unsolicited Business Proposal</u>

These are also called "marketing brochure" as earlier explained that these proposals are used just to introduce the product or services by the vendor initially. It does not contain specific information. The main aim to prepare this business proposal is to reach up to prospective customers. These are not designed to close a sale, but just to introduce the possibility of a sale.

COMPONENT OF BUSINESS PROPOSAL:

A good business proposal can achieve business heights. A proposal describes the description of a business in a summarized way. So, it says much in fewer words. The best elements of a business proposal that are must be included are:

- Executive Summary.
- Company's Description for Targeting Audience.
- Marketing and Sales Analysis.
- Competitive Analysis.
- Management Team Description.
- Financial Plan.
- Prospects and Procurement of Business.
- Request for Funding.
- Projection of Financial Assistance.

Executive Summary:

As the title says, this is the most essential and executive component for any business proposal. It highlights all the information on which other info and detail of the plan/ proposal depend. It includes the company's mission statement along with a short description for the audience.

Company's Description for Targeting Audience:

After preparation of the executive summary, a businessman prepares this section. In this section information regarding the company's policy, terms, services, products are described with well-focused customers/ audience. The target is to prepare this section to fulfill the aim. How an organization or company stands out as one and how the provided product/ service will be helpful to the audience.

Marketing and Sales Analysis:

The writer of business proposal outlines the marketing strategies and techniques of sales promotion by which he can achieve the target of the sale of product and services. This section reveals how a businessman implements the strategies including sales forecast, advertising, public relation etc. For this, the writer of a proposal can provide the testimonial from existing customers.

Competitive Analysis:

Competitive analysis is a statement of the business strategy. The purpose of this analysis is to determine the strength and weaknesses of the competitors of the same business that are running. The analysis of competitors can be done according to customer's point of view and company's strategy viewpoint. This analysis, in conjunction with an examination of unsuccessful companies and the reasons behind their failure, should provide a good idea about what key assets and skills are needed to be successful within a given industry and market segment. It is needed to establish this competitive advantage clearly so that the reader of the proposal understands not only how the company will accomplish its goal but also why the company's strategy will work.

Management Team Description:

This section is prepared keeping in mind the reader of proposal and how to influence them. Company's executives, managers, and personnel bios should be mentioned in such a manner that would help them to meet business goals. Experienced management team can get the faith of audience to perceive lower risk.

Financial Plan and Analysis:

This element includes the company's terms and policies regarding finance and financial assistance. It is the most important section because finance is the blood of all companies, and through this, a company can earn the profit. So, by this element, it should be discussed how a business will be able to utilize the customer fund by providing quality product/ services and will satisfy their expectations.

Prospects and Procurement of Business:

A proposal is a comprehensive roadmap for future planning of a business. This specifies the relevant information about future prospects like, how it works and what targets do a company has and how it will earn the profit.

Explanation of achievement is necessary to get the faith of the customers. In this element, a writer should mention all the attainments of the businesslike, patent, copyright, prototype, location of facility, registration, etc., that are essential for the development for the organization.

Request for Funding:

When a company needs funding from the public, to add this section becomes necessary. It is so that the company should explain the strategy of how a company will use funds that are invested by the people. A company discloses all the information regarding a project in a much-defined manner.

Projection of Financial Assistance:

This is the final section of a business proposal. This section includes the financial goal and expectations for the future that are analyzed based on market research. What annual projected earnings are there shall also be discussed.

So, above all elements are essential and must be kept in mind while preparing a proposal. It may vary up to some extent, depending on the need of a company.

HOW TO START WRITING A PROPOSAL?

When a person starts to think about writing a proposal, he draws a draft, the outlines that are essential for his objectives. Here, two things are to be remembered. One is, what things have to be taken care of before starting to write a proposal, and second is the steps while he starts to frame the proposal. Here, this process is divided into two ways:

i. Points to be remembered before starting to write a proposal.
ii. Steps to be taken while framing a proposal.

<u>Points to be remembered before starting to write a proposal</u>

- First of all, choose the audience and area in which you want to start working or that belongs to your interest and challenges you.
- Find out the right topic in which you are capable of doing work.
- Concise your work/ problem.
- Do research to find out the information regarding the research problem.
- Draw an outline for investigating the research problem.
- Make notes and organize them.

<u>Steps to be taken while framing a proposal</u>

The best way to write a proposal is to put all of the information in a concise and less descriptive way. It helps a writer to get what he wants. It is an idea to ask permission to execute or to get action on. It is a well-structured offer. A proposal generally consists of:

a. **Title-** It consists of the keywords for indexing. It is important because it defines the problem in brief. It should be short and simple, along with the keywords.

b. **Abstract-** It is of about 150-200 words. Basically, it is the summary of how the work would be carried forward and what are the objectives, scope, and expected outcome.

c. **Introduction-** It is a hook to start out the proposal. This makes sure a reader understands why this proposal is to be chosen. In this, the writer uses some background information to get the readers in the zone. A good hook should explain exactly what you could do for their business. A writer could make attractive promises like schemes, discount, offers, etc.

d. **State the Problem-** After the introduction, the proposal will set a body to discuss the purpose of the problem. In this section, it explains the reason and need of discussing the problem. Why it is worth looking for and how it is needed to understand to get the solution for the problem.

e. **Plan-** Plan helps in fixing the issue that is needful to convince the reader. In this, the writer discloses all the facts regarding the plan so that audience may take this seriously.

f. **Solution to the Problem-** This is written to convince the reader. It includes the proposed action whatever is beneficial for the proposed problem. It also includes the recommendation for the solution of the problem for the readers.

g. **Costs-** List of costs in a business proposal must be explained in the proposal. It can help out the reader to decide whether or not they would be able to afford a particular product/ services. In addition to this, the writer also should disclose additional financial benefit that will be received by the reader after making the purchase.

h. **Conclusion-** This is the final stage of a proposal. It restates the problem and the proposed solution. To encourage the reader to act on the proposal, it should end with a positive note.

<u>Things to remember while writing a proposal-</u>

- The proposal should be well-structured, well-researched, short, and simple.
- It assures that the rationale for the project is clear and carries worth.
- The means (methods) of completing the project are logical and well defined.
- The scope of the project is feasible regarding time frame and resources.

- The project and the proposal are thoughtful, reflective, and meaningful connecting with project future plans.
- Keep on focusing on those people who can be helped with the proposal and proposal writing.

Checklist after writing the proposal-

A writer must be assured about the information that he has written in the proposal before it reaches the audience:

- It has been carefully read, and it follows the instructions for completion of the grant or fellowship proposal.
- Writing is clear, concise, and grammatically correct.
- The order and structure of the presented proposal description follow that of writer's abstract.
- Corresponds about the budget has been outlined. Calculation & total of the proposed costs have also been checked for its accuracy.
- Objectives are clear, and the scope of the project is feasible.
- Proposed work should be explained in such a manner that individuals who do not have knowledge in this field can also understand.
- Carefully proofread and then share the proposal with others for clarity and accuracy.

Importance of writing a good proposal-

a. Plan for work- Proposal is a plan or an idea for the work to be done. It mentions the outlines and designs the way how a seller satisfies his buyer. It is helpful to quantify and analyze each hazard.
b. Justify the Claims- Through a proposal; the seller can justify the claims with extensive information that has been written in a proposal.
c. Provide Statistics- Proposal also provides statistical analysis of how a proposer will accomplish the objectives within time and cost what he has produced.
d. Communicates the Information- Proposal is an informative document. It is made in a way that it contains all that information that is useful to increase the sale and marketing of the product.
e. Solve the Problems- It explains explicitly how to meet out the requirement of a client what he wants to resolve.

f. Decrease Duplication- A proposal helps in decreasing the duplication of previously used information which is unavailable due to change with occupancy status.

g. Minimize the Risk- Risk can also be minimized through a good proposal because proposal manages the method in such a way to carry out the work done positively.

h. Improve awareness of employees- It outlines the steps, and include details of the actions taken to improve employee awareness and training is also provided accordingly.

a. A proposal can also be used as continuation, renewal or supplemental document.

PROJECT PROPOSAL

To understand the project proposal, this is necessary to know about the 'project', at first. Projects are unique kind of letters which creates the inimitable and special product and service. It is not long lasting, having specific objectives. It is clearly defined and describable. It would be better to say that project has a finite length and requires some amount of work to be performed. A successful project requires the end product or result to be well-understood before the project begins.

A project proposal is used early in the project life cycle to describe the project vision, timeframes, and deliverables so that to know what has to be done and by when. Also, delivers all the information that is needed for the success of completion of the project.

Project Proposal Tips-

- Keep it Simple/Estimate.
- Make a Hypothesis.
- Include an Appendix for extra information.
- Outline the Budget.
- Include deadlines and set realistic expectations about when stakeholders should expect to see results.
- Tailor it to whom you're writing for. Keep this in mind while drafting a proposal.

After approval of the proposal by that sponsor to whom it is written, the project proposal document would be useful. And then the project officially starts. According to the goal, it is needed to identify the correct format which is most appropriate for the respective audience; this can be a customer, a funding agency, or an end user. So, what makes a project unique, creating and delivering and makes it a good project proposal. Here many kinds of proposals are written according to their field.

- Basic Business Proposal
- Development Project Proposal
- Construction Project Proposal
- NGO Project Proposal
- Student Project Proposal
- Research Project Proposal
- Business Project Proposal
- Community Project Proposal

Sample Project Proposal for Funding-

1. Proposal summary

Proposal summary consists of two or three paragraphs summarising the key points or objectives of the project. It should have sufficient detail and specifics.

This section may be the last one that you complete as it is a synopsis of the entire proposal.

2. Introduction/overview of your business or organization

Here you include a biography of key staff, your business track record (success stories) institution goals and philosophy; essentially why your company should be selected for the proposed grant/research.

Include also all valid industry certifications (ISO or Quality Certifications), licences and business and indemnity insurance details.

You need to show that your company or organisation has the capacity and the ability to meet all deliverables form both an execution perspective but also meet all legal, safety and quality obligations.

3. Problem statement or Needs analysis/assessment

This is especially for the purpose of the grant proposals. In the problem statement, you explain who will benefit and how the solution will be implemented.

4. Project objectives

It includes details of the desired outcome and how success will be measured. This section is key to providing information on the benefits of grantee, community, and government.

Key performance indicators need to be articulated and explained with specific measurements details.

5. Project design

Skills needed for success, what additional facilities, transport and support services needed to deliver the project and defined measures for success. Good project management discipline and methodologies with detailed requirements specified and project schedule is a must.

6. Project evaluation

It covers product evaluation and process evaluation. Also, include the time-frame needed for evaluation and who will do the evaluation, including the specific skills.

7. Future funding / Self sustainability

This section of your grant proposal is for funding requirements that go beyond the project, total cost of ownership including ongoing maintenance, business, as usual, operational support and may require you to articulate the projected ongoing costs (if any) for at least 5 years.

An accurate cost model includes all factors including inflation, specialist skills, ongoing training, and potential future growth, decommissioning expenses when the project or the product reaches the end of life, all need to factor into this section.

8. Project budget

How much money is required to be funded to deliver the results? Provide full justification for all expenses including a table of services (or service catalogue). Remember that the project budget section is the true meat of your grant proposal.

Note- Additional tips for writing a grant proposal:

- You must have a good understanding of the proposed plan/ proposal.
- You should become closely familiar with all of the criteria related to the program for which a grant is being sought.
- Be a good project manager, know how to plan, lead, and deliver projects.
- Understand the organization that is providing the funds, understand their goals and align your proposal to them.

- Ensure that your idea or service is unique and not already funded by other government or private grants or is already implemented.
- Ensure that the benefits generated from the grant are tangible, measurable, benefit a wide spectrum of your community, and are a good value for the money invested.

<u>POINTS TO REMEMBER:</u>

- A proposal is an important document that ploughs the initial relationship between the organization and customers. The proposal frames the extensive information in a way that can achieve the goal to write this proposal. It is helpful to eliminate the stones by including the information.
- It can be defined as "A proposal is a document that is prepared for a prospective customer to persuade the prospect to adopt the solution to a problem or the fulfillment of a need in the proposal. Proposals are written for both private and public sector organizations."
- There is a difference between a proposal and writing a proposal. A proposal is an informative and important document having many types while writing a proposal is a thinking and persuasive process having many steps.
- A proposal plans for work justifies the claims and provides information to the readers. It solves the problem, decreases the duplication, and also minimizes the risk.
- Mainly, three types of business proposals are there like Formally Solicited Business Proposal, Informally Solicited Business Proposal, and Unsolicited Solicited Business Proposal. Business is of Request for Quotation (RFQ), Request for Proposal (RFP), Invitation for Bid (IFB), and Request for Information (RFI).
- Executive Summary, Company's Description for Targeting Audience, Marketing and Sales Analysis, Competitive Analysis, Management Team Description, Financial Plan, Prospects and Procurement of Business, Request for Funding, Projection of Financial Assistance are the main elements which are included in the business proposal.
- To start writing a proposal, it is important to think about the area of the problem, topic, gathering information, etc. first and then start writing. Remember that the writer of the proposal should follow the format according to his needs. Basically, title, abstract, introduction, state the

problem, solution of the problem, cost, qualification of the project is included in a format of business proposal and ends with a conclusion.

- Things to remember at the time writing a proposal: The project and the proposal should be thoughtful, reflective, meaningful, and well-defined connecting with project future plans.
- Checklist after writing the proposal is followed by the writer of the proposal like an assurance for the conciseness, correctness grammatically, budget, accuracy of totaling, etc.
- A project proposal is exactly a proposal which is helpful to convince the audience. It is a document prepared and takes the approval of the sponsor before commencing the project. Many types of proposals like development project student project research project business project proposal are there. It is meaningful and most important to identify the appropriate format of proposal.

CHAPTER SEVEN

REPORTS WRITING

INTRODUCTION

A report is written for a clear purpose and to a particular audience. In other words, reports are designed to record and convey information to the readers. Reports serve to document new information. Specific information and evidence are presented, analysed and applied to a particular problem or issue for specific audiences, goals, or functions. The type of report is often identified by its primary purpose, as in an accident report, a laboratory report, or a sales report.

Reports are often analytical or involve the rational analysis of information. Sometimes, they report the facts with no analysis at all. Other reports summarize past events, present current data, and forecast future trends. The information is presented in a structured format making use of sections and headings so that the information is easy to understand and follow.

An effective report presents and analyses facts and evidence that are relevant to the specific problem or issue of the report in brief. All sources used should be acknowledged and referenced throughout, under the preferred method of referencing.

NOTE- When preparing for the writing of your report, ask yourself the following questions-

- **What guidelines have you been given?**
- **What's the purpose of the report?**
- **What type of report is it?**
- **What do I need to show?**
- **What do I need to do?**

Many business professionals need to write a formal report at some point during their career, and some professionals write them regularly. Key decision-makers in business, education, and government use formal reports to make their important decisions. Several different organizational patterns may be used for formal report writing. However, all formal reports contain Title of the report, introductory material, and a body, supplementary items (discussions and recommendations). The introductory material is therefore critical to providing the audience with an overview and roadmap of the report. In contrast, the body of a formal report discusses the findings that lead to the recommendations. Above, is the sample process of formal report writing.

OBJECTIVES

After successful completion of this chapter, you will be able to-

- Understand the basics of report writing
- Understand various types of reports.
- Understand the structure of the reports.

TYPES OF REPORTS

Reports come in all sizes but are typically longer than a page and are somewhat shorter than a book. The type of report depends on its function, and different organizations have reports specific to them. For example, science researchers write lab reports, while incident reports are common in health-and-safety environments. Reports vary by function, organizational needs, and style. There are many types of reports discussed here:

- Lab Report- Communicates the procedures and results of laboratory activities.
- Research Report- Studies problems scientifically by developing hypotheses, collecting data, analysing data, and indicating findings or conclusions.
- Field Study Report- Describes one-time events, such as trips, conferences, seminars, as well as reports from branch offices, industrial and manufacturing plants.

- Incident or accident Report- Describes events such as accidents or altercations in the workplace to document them for legal and insurance purposes officially.
- Progress Report- Monitors and controls production, sales, shipping, service, or related business processes.
- Technical Report- Explains processes and products from a technical perspective.
- Financial Report- Analyses status and trends from a finance perspective.
- Case Study Report- Represents, analyses, and presents lessons learned from a specific case or example.
- Needs Assessment Report- Assesses the need for a service, product, project, program, or initiative.
- Comparative Advantage Report- Discusses competing products or services with an analysis of relative advantages and disadvantages.
- Feasibility Report- Analysis problems and predicts whether current solutions or alternatives will be practical, advisable, or produce the desired outcome(s).
- Instructional Report- Explains step-by-step instructions on the use of a product or service
- Compliance Report- Documents and indicates the extent to which a product or service is within established compliance parameters or standards.
- Cost-benefit Analysis Report- Analysis of the costs and benefits of products or services, including return-on-investment considerations.
- Recommendation Report- Makes recommendations to management and serves as a tool to solve problems and make executive decisions.

STRUCTURE OF A REPORT

The main features of a report are described below to provide a general guide. These should be used in conjunction with the instructions or guidelines provided by your organization as-

Cover Letter/transmittal letter[#] - It is either attached to the outside of the report with a paper clip or it is bound within the report. It is a communication from you (the report writer) to the recipient, the person/ organization who requested the report. The transmittal letter explains the context of the events that brought the report about. It contains information about the report (in very short) that does not belong in the report.

NOTE- # Transmittal letter is a brief letter or note sent with a document or parcel to explain the contents.

In the example of the transmittal letter in the following, notice the standard business-letter format. If you write an internal report, use the memorandum format instead; in either case, the contents and organization are the same as-

First paragraph- Cites the name of the report, putting it in italics. It also mentions the date of the agreement of writing the report.

Middle paragraph- Focuses on the purpose of the report and gives a brief overview of the report's contents.

Final paragraph- Encourages the reader to get in touch if there are questions, comments, or concerns. It closes with a gesture of goodwill, expressing hope that the reader finds the report satisfactory.

Title Page- This should briefly but explicitly describe the purpose of the report. Other details you may include submitted by, submitted to, the date and for whom the report is written.

Terms of Reference- Under this heading, you could include a brief explanation of who will read the report (audience) why it was written (purpose) and how it was written (methods). It may be in the form of a subtitle or a single paragraph.

Summary (Abstract) - The summary should briefly describe the content of the report. It should cover the aims of the report. The summary should provide the reader with a clear, helpful overview of the content of the report, just as outline or main points.

Contents (Table of Contents) - The contents page should list the different chapters and/or headings together with the page numbers. Your contents page should be presented in such a way that the reader can quickly scan the list of headings and locate a particular part of the report.

Acknowledgements- Where appropriate, you may wish to acknowledge the assistance of particular organizations or individuals who provided information, advice or help.

Glossary of Technical Terms- It is useful to provide an alphabetical list of technical terms with a brief, clear description of each term. You can also include in this section explanations of the acronyms, abbreviations or standard units used in your report.

Introduction- In the introduction part, the aim and objectives of the report should be explained in detail. Any problems or limitations in the scope of the report should be identified, and a description of research methods, the parameters of the research and any necessary background history should be included. In some reports, particularly in science subjects, separate headings for methods and results are used prior to the main body (Discussion) of the reports, as-

i. Methods- Information under this heading may include a list of equipment used, explanations of procedures followed, relevant information on materials used, including sources of materials, and details of any necessary preparation.
ii. Results- It includes a summary of the results of the investigation or experiment together with any necessary diagrams, graphs or tables of gathered data that support your results.

Discussion- The main body of the report is where you discuss your material. The facts and evidence you have gathered should be analyzed and discussed with specific reference to the problem or issue. If your discussion section is lengthy, you might divide it into section headings.

Conclusion- In the conclusion, you should show the overall significance of what has been covered. You may want to remind the reader of the most important points that have been made in the report or highlight what you consider to be the most central issues or findings. However, no new material should be introduced in conclusion.

Appendix- Under this heading includes all the supporting information you have used that is not published. This might include tables, graphs, questionnaires, surveys or transcripts.

ESSENTIAL STAGES TO WRITE UP THE REPORT

All reports need to be clear, concise and well structured. The key to writing an effective report is to allocate time for planning and preparation. With careful planning, the writing of a report will be made much easier.

Stage 1: Understanding the report in brief

You need to understand the purpose of your report as described in your report brief or instructions. Consider who the report is for and why it is being written.

Stage 2: Gathering and selecting information

Here, you need to begin to gather relevant information. Your information may come from a variety of sources, but how much information you will need will depend on how much detail is required in the report. Keep referring to your report brief to help you decide what relevant information is.

Stage 3: Organizing your material

Begin by grouping together points that are related. These may form sections or chapters. Choose an order for your material that is logical and easy to follow.

Stage 4: Analyzing your material

It is not enough to simply present the information you have gathered; you must relate it to the problem or issue described in the report brief.

Stage 5: Writing the report

Having organized your material into appropriate sections and headings, you can begin to write the first draft of your report. You may find it easier to write the summary and contents page at the end when you know exactly what will be included.

<u>Here you may plan for-</u>

- To introduce the main idea of the chapter/section/paragraph. To explain and expand the idea, defining any key terms.
- To present the relevant evidence to support your point(s).
- To comment on each piece of evidence showing how it relates to your point(s).
- To conclude your chapter/section/paragraph by either showing its significance to the report as a whole or making a link to the next chapter/section/paragraph.

Stage 6: Reviewing and redrafting

Ideally, you should leave time to take a break before you review your first draft. Be prepared to rearrange or rewrite sections in the light of your review. Try to read the draft from the perspective of the reader. It is easy to follow with a clear structure that makes sense.

Stage 7: Presentation

If you are satisfied with the content and structure of your redrafted report, you can turn your attention to the presentation.

REPORT WRITING CHECKLIST

In the process of writing a good report, you should always be careful about the following-

- Plan the stages of your research well and writing the report carefully.
- Report considers the audience's needs; write with the reader in mind at all times.
- Do your research – the groundwork for your report.
- Format should reflect institutional norms and expectations.
- Information should accurate, complete, and documented.
- Keep very accurate records of all of your findings.
- Information should easy to read and understand.
- Terms should clearly define.
- Figures, tables, and art support written content as well.
- Figures, tables, and art should clear and correctly labeled.
- Figures, tables, and art should easily understandable without text support.
- Words should easy to read (font size, arrangement and organization).
- Results should be clear and concise.
- Report precisely and evaluate honestly.
- Recommendations should be reasonable and well-supported.
- Study examples of similar reports to understand the correct style and content to use.
- Report should represent your best effort.
- Report speaks for itself without your clarification or explanation.
- Write clear references for all quotations and source material you have been used in your report.

POINTS TO REMEMBER:

- Reports are designed to record and convey information to the readers.
- The type of report is often identified by its primary purpose, as in an accident report, a laboratory report, or a sales report.
- An effective report presents and analyses facts and evidence that are relevant to the specific problem or issue of the report in brief.
- The type of report depends on its function, and different organizations have reports specific to them.

<u>GLOSSARY:</u>

- **Progress Report**- Monitors and controls production, sales, shipping, service, or related business processes.
- **Research Report**- Studies problems scientifically by developing hypotheses, collecting data, analyzing data, and indicating findings or conclusions.
- **Case Study Report**- Represents, analyses, and presents lessons learned from a specific case or example.
- **Compliance Report**- Documents and indicates the extent to which a product or service is within established compliance parameters or standards.

- **Transmittal Letter**- The transmittal letter explains the context of the events that brought the report about. It contains information about the report (in very short) that(letter) does not belong in the report.

CHAPTER EIGHT

LETTER WRITING

INTRODUCTION

Writing skill is an essential part of communication as it allows an individual to transfer his/her thoughts, ideas, suggestions and opinions in an effective way. Good writing skill is part and parcel of life, as it helps an individual to embark their career professionally. Well- refined writing skills are needed at administration, business, management, negotiations, legal presentations, etc. Writing skills comprises the adequate format, style, diction and layout. Everything you write should be well-tailored in a structured way so it will be deciphered easily.

In today's era, every business or administrative activities is executed only by the means of communication. This will be not an exaggeration if we call communication is the life-blood of business. A good written communication shows one's credibility with his work.

OBJECTIVES

After successful completion of this unit, you will be able to-

- Understand the importance of Letter writing.
- Learn different styles of Letters.
- Differentiate between Biodata, Curriculum Vitae (CV) and Resume.
- Learn the format of Biodata, Curriculum Vitae (CV) and Resume.

LETTER WRITING

Letter writing constitutes the most important role in written communication. A letter is a written message that can be handwritten or typed. Letters whether formal or informal have some sort of format and layout. An individual should adherently follow the rules and regulations for writing letters. This helps the receiver to comprehend the information in the desired manner by the sender.

Every individual must have some basic writing skill, as this is the most important part of communication skill. Anywhere in life weather an individual is related to academics or business, must possess the knowledge of good writing. Business or any other field requires good writers; even the digital age has not reduced the need for writing. Like online conversation chats, e-mail, reports, website updates marketing, advertising, etc. all these requires excellent writing skill.

Importance of letter writing-

- It is an effective way of communication.
- It has credibility and legality.
- It is useful regarding complaints, requests, marketing, negotiating, etc.
- It is useful for academic field. For e.g. research paper, research proposal, etc.
- It is useful for administrative field. For e.g. complaint and request letters, government schemes execution letters, etc.
- It is used for business field. For e.g. business letters of agreement, proposals, negotiations, etc.
- It also fosters an individual to share their refine ideas to others.
- It also helps an individual to showcase their writing skill at the time of writing job- application and resume.

- Letters can be formal and informal, but they convey a sense of responsible attitude of sharing information towards the receiver.
- Good letter writing improves the company's image towards the public interest.

Effective ways of writing letters-

- Firstly, follow the accurate format and layout for writing any letter.
- Mention the correct address followed by the proper salutation in regards to the receiver.
- Begin the letter with positive vibes with well-knitted sentences.
- State properly the motive of writing a letter.
- Organize your important information in points.
- Do not use highly embellish words as it will create ambiguity.
- Avoid using technical jargons if the letter is for the layman.
- The content of the letter should be properly tailored and ideas should not be fragmented.
- Conclusion of the letter should be there that consist the gist of the letter.
- Complimentary close of the letter must be followed by full name and designation of the sender.
- Formal letters and demi-official letters should be followed by copy notations if needed as they make letters more effective.
- Avoid using idioms and phrases while writing official letters as it reduced the effectiveness of it.

FORMAL LETTERS

Formal letters are those letters which have set defined rules and regulation. These letters have impersonal tone and formal content. Formal letters especially are written for the formal communication such as communication at office, organizations, companies, etc. totally professional in nature.

Formal letters are written for official purposes to authorities, dignitaries, colleagues, seniors etch and not to personal contact or family members. These letters hold specific format and layout, which gives them a professional touch as well as make formal communication effective.

Format of Formal Letters-

Well-cultivated formal letters tone should be serious but not complex. In formal letters, content is literal in nature and to the point. To write effective formal letters, an individual should adhere to the basic pattern mentioned below.

- Sender's Address
- Date
- Receiver's Address
- Subject of the letter
- Salutation
- Main body [i- Introduction of the matter, ii- Explanation of the matter, iii- conclusion]
- Complimentary close.

<u>Let's detail the parts of a formal letter:</u>

- **Sender's Address**- Address of the sender with detail like Name, Title, company, e-mail, contact no, city, state and postal code.
- **Date**- undated letters gives a bad impression. The date should always be written in full. A date can be written with two different styles. Example- DD/MM/YY or MM/DD/YY
- **Receiver's Address**- Address of the receiver should be written at left side after the date. It consists of the full and clear address of the recipient preceded by the courtesy title like 'Mr.' or 'Ms.'
- **Subject**- It gives a brief introduction of the content of the letter. It should be written in one line. The subject of the letter should be bold and underline.
- **Salutation**- If you know the recipient's name, you can write like Dear Mr. XYZ or Dear Dr ABC and if not aware with the name, Dear Sir/ Madam. If there are two recipients or more than two, we address them like Dear Messrs. Alex and smith Lambert / Dear Messrs.
- **Main body**- It is the most important component of the business letter. The main body of the letter has three part of division:

  i. Introduction – This part of the letter tells the main purpose of writing.
  ii. Explanation – This part elaborates relevant details concerning purpose of I paragraph.

iii. Conclusion – The last paragraph concluded the relevant details as well as talk about the actions of the recipient expected by the sender.

- **Complimentary close**- It is mandatory to end the letter politely by using a complimentary close. The most common closes are "yours faithfully/yours sincerely". It is also followed by the signature, name and designation of the sender.

Do's at the time of writing Formal letters-

- Firstly, the foremost thing to write a formal letter effectively is to adhere to format and layout.
- The content of the formal letter should to be the point and specific in nature.
- Addresses of the sender and recipient's must be clearly written.
- There will be no comma followed by the salutation, Sir.
- Proper line spacing should be given at the time of writing a letter.
- Outlook of the letter should be neat and clean.
- Main body of the paragraph should be properly divided into Introduction, main speech and conclusion.
- Complimentary close like Yours faithfully/Yours sincerely; in this, there will be no apostrophes at yours.
- All the parts of a formal letter aligned to left margin.
- Subject of the letter should be underlined and bold.

Don'ts at the time of writing Formal letters-

- Don't be careless at the time of writing recipient's name, title, gender, and designation.
- Do not use fragmented ideas as it leads to create ambiguity.
- Do not use decorated words and highly embellished phrases.
- Don't commit grammar and spelling error as it gives a wrong impression to the reader.

- Do not use slang, jargons, and colloquial language.
- Do not use personal pronoun, i.e. I, you, we.
- Do not write letters in the passive voice.
- Do not use long sentences as it sometimes diverted the real meaning.
- Do not rely so much on spell-check. Always proofread before sending the letter.
- Do not make formal letters colorful and choose font style aptly.

INFORMAL LETTERS

Informal letters are mainly used for personal communication. They are personal in tone, non- serious in nature and casual in conversation. They are written to close acquaintances, relatives, family members, etc. Thus, they do not have a specific format and layout which one to adhere to it. They can be written as per the writer's wishes and the requirement of the situation.

Informal letters are flexible in nature. The subject matter of these letters is full of affection and conversation in tone. In these letters, you can use your personal slang language. There is no rigidity over the choice of words and phrases.

Informal Letter Format-

As we mentioned above, that there is no set format for writing an Informal letter. But some general conventions have to be followed. We will be looking at the general pattern to write effective and impressive Informal letters.

- Sender's Address
- Receiver's Address (optional)
- Date
- Main body- [i] Introduction [ii] Explanation [iii] conclusion

Let's detail the parts of formal letter:

- Sender's Address: Address of the sender should be located at the right or left corner. It is necessary to provide full address with a name, street name, city, zip code, country, etc so it helps the recipient to make a reply.

- Receiver's Address: This part is optional as the receiver's address is also written on the envelope.
- Date: The date is mentioned below the address after one-line spacing. It is customary as it allows the receiver to know when the letter has written.
- Main Body: Usually, the main body is divided into three parts-

  i. Introduction: Informal letters start with great warmth and a casual tone. Begin with asking or showing concern towards the recipient. Example-

  > Hope you are doing good.
  > It's been a while when I have heard you.
  > I hope this letter finds you in the best of spirits.

  i. Central Body: In this part, the main intention of writing a letter is revealed in the most unofficial and conversational tone.
  ii. Conclusion: It is the closing part of the letter where the writer summarises and bid goodbye with affection. Example-Hope to see you soon, etc.
  iii. Closing: At last writer close the letter with affectionate phrases like- Yours Lovingly, Lots of Love, Yours Affectionately. These closings are followed by the writer's name.

DEMI-OFFICIAL LETTERS

In general term, Demi-official letter is defined as the letter that communicates official correspondence along with personal news is called Demi-official letter or Demi-government letter. These letters are official letters that help attain official objective through personal relationship known as demi-official letters. These letters are less formal than formal letters. There are no strict rules to be followed in drafting such letters.

As these letters are more flexible in nature because of their language, writing style, and presentation, thus, it is practiced widely in communication. However, this letter includes both personal and official information, so it is written for the particular receiver not in a generalized way. People holding the same authority and status usually exchanged this type of letters.

Features of Demi-official Letters-

- Purposes: The main purpose of a demi-official letter is to serve some personal affairs along with official matters. To attain an official objective through personal relationships is the purpose of the demi-official letter. This letter is written to exchange business information with a personal touch.
- Language: It is written in such a language that has a personalized tone. Such a letter can be written through personal gestures for which language seems to be very simple and clear.
- Nature: Its nature is flexible. It is administrative, commerce, and business oriented. It is moderately big in size compared to the formal letters.
- Status: This letter is exchanged among the people who possess the same status. In this letter, the person who writes the letter is quite familiar to the recipient's status in a friendly way, thus the language is casual and less formal.
- Structure: Demi-official letter does not follow any specific structure. It follows the basic pattern of formal letters, but the language is friendly and away from structured content. It cannot be classified as an official letter.
- Copy: No carbon copy is initiated for these letters as they are written to a specific recipient.
- Salutation and complimentary close: Use of salutation and complimentary close depend on a personal relationship between the sender and receiver.
- Appeal: Its appeal is limited to the specific individual only.
- Enclosure: Use of enclosure in such a letter is a rare case as it belongs to a specific individual.

Attributes of Demi-official letters-

- To succeed in an official objective through personal relationships is the reason for the demi-official letter.
- If the subject matter is confidential in nature, then this type of letter is helpful.
- Its nature is versatile, i.e. combination of personal and official. It is moderately large in size.
- Such a letter can be written through a personal touch for which language seems to be very simple.
- Avoid needless obtrusion by other people and avoid the delay that may be caused by custom official communication.
- It is usually addressed by the name and title of the person who is thought to attend to the focus subject of the letter.
- Salutation normally starts with 'My Dear X' 'Dear Mr./Mrs. Y'
- The appropriate manner of a subscription is 'Yours sincerely'
- Such a letter is signed by the officer concerned and not by someone else on behalf of the officer.
- Generally, these letters don't contain carbon copy and enclosure.
- Content of the letter has the tint of personal tone with official information.

BUSINESS LETTERS

Business letters are one of the most essential means of communication in the business world. Due to the vast expansion of commerce and trade, the importance of letters has increased. A well-written and structured letter represents the business identity as well as conveys the professionalism of a company.

Business letters can be written for various commercial purposes such as business deal, complaint, warning, notice, invitation, declaration, information, apology, and various other corporate matters.

Nowadays, business operations are not restricted to any state or nation, all over the world there are numbers of organisations big and small. All types of exchange of goods and materials or any other thing require documentation; business letters is one amongst such documentation. Business letters are the cheapest and most extensive form of communication used all over the world.

Different kinds of business letter-

Correspondence is an integral part of commerce to exchange ideas, thoughts and opinions with others. There are different kinds of business letters, but they follow a generalised pattern with different subject-matter. They are the principal source of business communication which helps in the growth of the trade and establishing bonding among business partners.

- Sales letter
- Business inquiry letter
- Quotation letter
- Order letter
- Complaint letter
- Recovery letter
- Letters of goodwill
- Collection letters
- Bank and insurance correspondence
- Correspondence with media and government offices

Parts of a business letter-

Each business letters have fixed components which can be described as parts of the business letter. Each component adds to an overall impact which the letter makes over the reader. The parts of the business letters are as follows-

- Letter head / Heading
- The reference
- Date
- The inside name and address
- Salutation
- Subject
- The body paragraphs
- Complimentary close
- Signature

- Enclosures
- Copies

Key concern at the time of writing business letters-

- Good composition is essential in business correspondence.
- Highly decorated words such as proverb and poetry have no place at writing business letter.
- Avoid long phrases, idioms, and assumptions.
- Each sentence must be simple, clear, accurate, complete and clean.
- If there is a lot of information to be stated, the letter may be divided into paragraphs and written step by step.
- Letter should be error free means no grammatical and spelling mistakes.
- Use active not passive voice.

- Main body must be divided into: Introduce, say and summarize.
- Print business letter on standard sized paper.
- Write a business letter on a letterhead.
- Subject matter of business letter must be adhering to the information.
- Unnecessary jargons should not be used.
- Language should be formal and straightforward.
- Follow the correct format and layout.
- Enclosure and carbon copy should be used when necessary.

JOB APPLICATION COVER LETTER

A letter of a job application, also known as a cover letter is a document sent with your resume to provide additional information about your skills and experience to the recruiter. The letter of application is intended to provide detailed information on the candidate's eligibility for the job.

Your resume's cover letter is one of the strongest tools in your job hunt. It can strengthen a weak resume, distinguish you from boring job candidates, and help you make a connection with the hiring manager that would otherwise be impossible. A cover letter (also known as a covering letter or application letter) is a one-page document that introduces a job seeker's work history, professional skills, and personal interest in applying for a job. Your cover letter should include relevant professional experience, a persuasive matter, and avoid basic spelling and grammar mistakes.

Key points of job application cover letters:

- Include relevant information regarding your qualification and work experience.
- The appeal of the letter should be eye-catching.
- Present yourself in an impressive tone.
- A cover letter should be totally related with the job requirement.
- End your letter with a reason for the recruiter to contact you.
- A cover letter should not be exceeded one page in length.
- A good conclusion that reiterates your interest in the job.
- Include brief-introduction of your key traits which are useful for the job.
- Avoid using exaggeration words as it leads to a negative impact.
- Sign off the cover letter by mentioning all the contact details.

BIO-DATA, CURRICULUM VITAE (CV) AND RESUME

Biodata, CV and Resume are the three terms used to express the profile of an individual. All these three consist of their own personal traits, though closely related but are different in nature. They are the documents highlighting skills, education, and experience that a candidate submits when applying for a job.

To bring out from the confusion, these are the differences between "Resume, CV and Bio- data".

Bio-Data

Bio-data means biographical data. It is short and comprises general information like name, date of birth, religion, gender, marital status, nationality, and educational qualification. It is an old version of resume and CV. Its data comprises only in one page with the basic information. It is generally outdated for seeking a job as it comprises less information of the candidate.

Resume

Resume is a word that originated from the French word means summary. Education, skills & employment summarized together is called a Resume. A resume generally starts with the career objective, followed by education qualification, project details, major skills, internships, workshops, strengths, interests, personal details, etc. Usually, it consists of details about a person, broken into bullets & written in active voice and subjective details. A resume should not exceed more than 2 pages, but it should also be not less than 1 page. It is best used to advertise your professional profile in the corporate world.

Curriculum Vitae (CV)

CV can be defined as curriculum vitae. It is a Latin word meaning "Course of Life". As the meaning suggests, it consist all the details of an individual in an elaborated manner. It consists of information like qualification, job description, and specification, technical skills in detail, hobbies, strengths, weakness, rewards, etc each in detail as you are describing the summary of your life. It should be of at least 2 to 3 pages. It could also exceed more than 3 pages depending upon one's experience. It covers all details in chronological order. It is more popular in corporate at international level. CVs are mainly used to applying for – international job, health care, research, academic, teaching, scholarships, apprenticeships, fellowships, internships, and scientific jobs.

<u>POINTS TO REMEMBER:</u>

- Writing skill is an essential part of communication as it allows an individual to transfer their thoughts, ideas, suggestions and opinions in an effective way. Good writing skill is part and parcel of life, as it helps an individual to embark their career professionally.
- A letter is a written message that can be handwritten or typed. Letters whether formal or informal have some sort of format and layout.
- Formal letters are written for official purposes to authorities, dignitaries, colleagues, seniors, etc and not to personal contact or family members.

- Informal letters are mainly used for personal communication.
- In general term, Demi-official letter is defined as the letter that communicates official correspondence along with personal news is called demi-official letter or demi- government letter.
- Bio-data means biographical data.
- Resume is a word originated from the French word means summary. Education, skills & employment summarized together is called a Resume.
- Curriculum Vitae (CV) can be defined as a Latin word meaning is "Course of Life". As the meaning suggests, it consist all the details of an individual in elaborated manner. It consists of information like qualification, job description, and specification, technical skills in detail, hobbies, strengths, weakness, rewards, etc each in detail as you are describing the summary of your life.

GLOSSARY:

- **Bio-data**- Biographical data.
- **CV**- Curriculum Vitae.
- **Business Letter**- Most essential means of communication in the business world.
- **Demi-official letter**- A letter that communicates official correspondence along with personal news is called demi-official letter or demi-government letter.
- **Informal Letter**- Mainly used for personal communication, non-serious in nature and casual in conversation.
- **Formal Letter**- A letter with set defined rules and regulation. These letters have impersonal tone and formal content; specially written for formal communication such as communication at office, organizations, companies, etc.

CHAPTER NINE

E-Skills

(TELEPHONE AND E-MAIL COMMUNICATION)

INTRODUCTION:

Telephones are devices that allow the user to communicate messages across lines electronically. Alexander Graham Bell invented the first telephone in 1876 in Boston. It is difficult to estimate the total number of telephones that exists today. They are ubiquitous (present everywhere) because of their extreme importance as a communications tool.

Telephone skills become important as technology and equipment change rapidly. Good communication skills will always be highly essential when using the telephone. Evolving technology will enhance the use of telephone in the future. Effective telephone skills are predicated on strong communications skills. Telephone etiquette refers to the principles of behaviour that one should use during a telephone conversation.

An e-mail is a digital message sent electronically from one computer or device to other computers or devices. E-mail or "electronic mail," is one of the most widely used features of the Internet, along with the web. Ray Tomlinson is universally known as the creator of e-mail as part of a program for ARPANET (Advanced Research Projects Agency Network) in 1971.

Videsh Sanchar Nigam Limited (VSNL) in India, launched the country's first public internet service on 14th August 1995, and thereafter e-mail become an essential part in our life.

E-mail is information stored on a computer that is exchanged between two or more users over internet. More precisely we can say e-mail is a message that may contain text, files, images, or other attachments sent through a network to an individual or group of individuals.

E-mail etiquette refers to the principles of behaviour that one should use when writing or answering e-mail messages. E-mail etiquette depends upon the person to whom you are writing: friends & relatives, partners, customers, superior or subordinates, etc. It is also known as the code of conduct for e-mail communication.

There are pros and cons for both telephone and e-mail communication. The most important thing is the context, i.e. why you need to communicate, and what you are communicating. Some things are best discussed through e-mail, and some are best though the phone.

OBJECTIVES:

After successful completion of this chapter, you will be able to-

- Understand, explain and define telephone as well as e-mail communication.
- Describe the different characteristics of telephone communication.
- Write e-mail in an attractive and efficient manner.
- Understand the etiquette for telephone and e-mail communication.

TELEPHONE SKILL

Telephones are devices that allow the user to communicate messages across lines electronically. One can easily communicate with those both nearby and far away using a telephone by simply dialling a specially designated number. The word telephone comes from two Greek words meaning "far" and "sound."

Handling the wide variety of both incoming and outgoing telephone calls requires in-depth skill. Customer service is an extremely important aspect of telephone skills. Good customer service via the telephone shows respect for the customer and builds business and relationships. Good customer service is provided by maintaining an excellent voice quality that is easy to understand and includes a pleasant tone spoken at a reasonable speed. Selecting appropriate vocabulary is also important. If words are used that are not understood, positive communication will not be conveyed.

An efficient business telephone streamlines good communication between organization and customers. A telephone offers a faster interaction than e-mail, is more personal, easy, and quick to use. We must follow some telephone skills in our daily life for better communication. The details of such skills are described here.

Basic Telephone Skills-

The basic telephone skills include appropriate methods for calling, answering calls, transferring calls, putting calls on hold, taking messages, and recording voice mail messages, etc. Here are some very common questions that we can ask ourselves during a telephone call.

- How to communicate effectively on the telephone,
- How to talk to customers,
- How professionally we need to talk.

Effective Communication-

Here are some basic skills, we need to follow for communicating effectively on the telephone:

Skill 1: Answer the phone specifying who you are.

Start your call with three parts greetings. The three parts are: the buffer words, the company or department name and your name.

A pleasant buffer phrase such as "Good Morning," or "Thank you for calling XYZ Company," sets the stage for the call. Follow that buffer phrase with the name of the company or department and then your name.

Skill 2: Speak clearly.

Before you make the phone call, think about the purpose of the call. For example, do you want to gather information, communicate information, negotiate, obtain agreement, make arrangements, sell something, or develop an idea? Always talk clearly and be specific during telephone calls. Long sentences do not always show fluency. Throughout the telephone call, try to bring your ideas across in a structured way. Do not be tempted to hop from one subject to another; even new ideas come into your mind.

Skill 3: Use words that make sense to the other person.

Messages may also be conveyed in the way the words are delivered. If you sound bored, angry or disinterested, the other person may well pick up on it, and it will then be irrelevant how good your proposal is or how valid your arguments are. It is true that they cannot see you, but a lot can be communicated through your tone of voice, so make sure that it matches the message that you are trying to get across.

Good customer service is provided by maintaining an excellent voice quality that is easy to understand and includes a pleasant tone spoken at a reasonable speed. Selecting appropriatevocabulary is also important. If words used are not understood, positive communication will not be conveyed. Listen carefully when servicing a customer. Be prepared to offer responses that will be delivered in a positive manner.

Skill 4: Use good, descriptive language during the conversation.

A key difference between professional and personal phone calls is obvious, i.e. the language. It might be acceptable to use slang and swears when talking on the phone with your close friends, but never use such types of language with customers as you may lose your customers forever. Always be mindful and respectful with your customer during phone calls. You never know what customers might be offended by something you say, so it is best to use formal language. It is okay to throw in humour if appropriate, but never crack a joke that could upset a customer.

Skill 5: Write down important points before making a call.

It is an excellent idea to write down the important points or any questions prior the call or during the call. During the call, when both parties are asking questions, it is equally important to listen attentively. Attentive listening can be demonstrated by speaking in such a way that the listener knows you are hearing.

Skill 6: Repeat important points during a call.

This is actually a good idea in any situation. Especially if you are communicating on the telephone, or in another language, there will be times when you are not sure about something that the other person said. It could be because they have not been clear. Maybe there was background noise. It could be that they were speaking quickly, or they have a regional accent. The reason does not matter. It is always better to ask for clarification than to guess what the other person meant, or to be unsure about what they think or are going to do. It is also better to repeat and clarify important points during the telephone call.

Communication with Customer-

Our communications with the customer over telephone have a great impact on our business as well as personal life. Here are some basic skills that we need to follow while talking to any customer over telephone:

Skill 1: Practice active listening skills. Never argue or interrupt the customer.

The four major means of communication are speaking, reading, writing, and listening, with listening being the most important part. Listening involves sensing, interpreting, evaluating, and responding.

Use a combination of different words and short phrases to acknowledge that you heard and understand what the caller has said. Spoken feedback signals are even more important on the phone than face-to-face. Without them, customers wonder if you are listening or not. If you are adding notes on the computer, tell the caller, so they know the typing sound they hear is related to their call.

Skill 2: Lower your voice and speak in an even tone.

A positive tone and friendly voice can encourage comfort in the caller. Starting a conversation with a pleasant greeting sets the tone for the whole phone call. Answering in a rushed or annoyed manner puts a negative impact on the conversation, leading it in the wrong direction. The thing you want is for your caller, especially someone who is particularly helpless, like a patient facing a medical emergency, to feel even more nervous or anxious than they already are.

People do not just communicate with their words. Messages are also conveyed in the way that words are delivered. If you sound bored, angry or disinterested, the other person may well pick up on it, and it will then be irrelevant how good your proposal is or how valid your arguments. It is true that they cannot see you, but a lot can be communicated through your tone of voice, so make sure that it matches the message that you are trying to get across.

Skill 3: Establish rapport through empathy.

Empathy is "the ability to understand and share the feelings of another". Rapport is "a close and harmonious relationship in which the people or groups concerned understand each other's feelings or ideas and communicate well". Rapport is all about highlighting common interests and establishing a mutual feeling of friendliness. When people like each other, whether in business, friendship, or both, they tend to help each other.

Here are three ways you can increase your rapport rating with prospects and customers:

Match your customer's style: Pay attention to how your customer prefers to communicate and get in step. Does your customer prefer to get right down to business, or warm up by engaging in small talk? What kinds of things does he or she find funny, interesting, or exciting? If your customer talks quickly and loudly, make an effort to match that energy.

Trust builds rapport: Your customers will learn to trust you if you fulfil your promise. Keep your commitments, call when you say you will, and always follow through. Be careful not to make promises you might not be able to keep. Too many salespeople make well- intentioned commitments, only to find they are unable to find time to fulfil them. They may not always lose a sale because of this, but they are certainly not building the kind of trust that will make that customer anxious to give referrals.

Another way to build trust is to demonstrate that you are interested in their well-being, beyond your own profit potential. Know and appreciate your customer's needs beyond your product. See what you can do to help them meet those needs. Little things like finding information for them or putting them in touch with other suppliers, tend to make a big difference.

Practice reciprocity: When you treat people in a certain way, they tend to want to treat you in the same way. Find ways to treat your customers as valued members of your professional and even social circle. In life and in business, the little things make a big difference.

Skill 4: Avoid getting upset or angry.

There are various reasons why customers become angry. Your product or service is not always what is specifically upsetting to them. Angry customers could be under great stress, having trouble at work, experiencing family issues or be facing some other life challenge. Avoid the impulse to talk over them, even if you have good news when you find the caller or customer is in a different mood.

Here are some tips for answering and handling calls professionally:

Tips 1: Promptly answer calls. The average ring takes 6 seconds.

Tips 2: Be warm and welcoming.

Tips 3: Introduce yourself and your business.

Tips 4: Speak clearly.

Tips 5: Do not use slang or buzz words.

Tips 6: Ask before you put people on hold.

<u>Advanced Telephone Skills-</u>

Advanced telephone skills will allow you to develop the core skills of being able to influence

on the telephone and further build rapport with your clients or customers. Develop the confidence needed to have that difficult conversation and get your own way. Here we will discuss some advanced telephone skills for better communication over the telephone with customers. Here are ten simple yet crucial reminders for delivering exceptional customer service on the phone.

Skill 1: Answering a Business Call

Start your business call with any one of three buffer phrases as per timing. Pick up the phone in time and after the greeting introduce yourself and your company. When answering a business phone, it is important that it is not allowed to ring more than three times. Advise employees that the second or third ring is the ideal time to pick up the telephone.

The phone should be answered with a positive greeting such as "Hello," "Good Morning," or "Good Afternoon," etc. Following the greeting the person who answers the phone should give his or her name and the name of the business or organization that is being contacted.

Put on a smile before placing or answering a phone call. Whenever a person smiles, it affects the sound of his or her voice and gives a more pleasant and friendly tone. For clarity, the telephone should be held a distance of two fingers from the mouth.

Speak in a clear tone using a voice that is neither too loud nor too low. Words should be enunciated and said slow enough that people are able to understand what is being said to them. When a caller is speaking, listen to what he or she has to say without interruptions. Skill Example:

(You) "Good Morning, "Good Afternoon" or "Good Evening".

Skill 2: Putting a Caller on Hold

If someone must be put on hold, ask for permission first and give him or her option to leave a voice-mail message. When taking them off of hold, thank the caller to show that their time is respected. Be sure to let the caller know why you need to put them on hold, ask if they are able to hold and then wait for a response. Callers hate being ordered to hold with no control over the situation. If the caller is not able to hold, handle their needs by offering options, such as a call back.

Skill Example:

(You) "I'll need some time to pull up that information from the system and it might take few minutes. Are you able to hold?"

(Caller's Response) "Yes, thanks!"

Skill 3: Thanking the Caller for Holding

When a caller has to be put on hold or gets dumped immediately into a hold queue when they call, it is very frustrating. You can ease that frustration and put the call on a positive path by thanking the customer for holding. This reconnects with callers and puts the conversation back on a positive path.

Skill Example:

(You) "Thank you for holding".

Skill 4: Monogramming the Call

People enjoy hearing their name, so using it helps set a positive tone for the call. Using the caller's name and saying it correctly is an efficient way of letting them know that you intend to assist. Do not be afraid to ask for help with pronunciation and spelling. It signals to the caller that you are willing to take time to give good service.

Skill Example A:

(Caller's Request) "Hi. My name is Chris Dixon, and I need to change an order I placed yesterday."

(Your Response) "Sure, Chris, I'll be happy to help you. My name is Karen. What do you need to be changed?"

Skill Example B: (Caller's Request) "Yes, would you please tell him that Bob Rebzinski called?"

(Your Response) "I'm sure a lot of people misspell your last name, and I don't want to be one of them. Would you please spell your name?"

Skill 5: Avoiding Excuses

Callers want solutions, not excuses. What excuses annoy customers the most? Things like, "Our computers are down" or "Sorry, but that's our policy." Take responsibility for all the calls you answer and tell your callers that you intend to help. If you receive the first contact with the customer, take 100% of the responsibility to guide the caller to a place where there will be a resolution. Rather than telling a customer, "That's not my department,".

Skill Example:

(Caller's Request) "This is Mr Whitfield. I have some questions about the invoice I received."

(Your Response) "Hi Mr Whitfield. Thanks. You're actually going to need to speak with Keisha in our billing department. I'm in the service area, but I can go ahead and connect you, and, just in case we get disconnected, Keisha's extension is 292. Are you able to hold?"

(Caller's Reply) "Sure."

Skill 6: Giving Spoken Feedback Signals

Use a combination of different words and short phrases to acknowledge that you heard and understand what the caller has said. Be sure to mirror back some of what the caller has said. Spoken feedback signals are even more important on the phone than face-to-face. Without them, customers wonder if you are listening, if they have been disconnected or if you are even able to help them. If you are adding notes on the computer, tell the caller, so they know the typing sound they hear is related to their call.

Skill Example:

(Caller's Request) "I'd like to have my things packed up by your movers on the 23rd in the morning.

(Your Response) "Good. I'm jotting this down. All right. Got it. Pack on the 23rd in the morning." (Caller Continues) "Right. We'll need the packers to come in first and pack my dishes. So, they need to be very careful when they pack my dishes."

(Your Response) "Sure. I understand. I'll mark that on the order: Be very careful when we pack the dishes."

(Caller's Reply) "Good. Thanks for being so thorough. I appreciate it."

Skill 7: Being Prepared

It is a good practice to keep paper and a pen or pencil next to your phone at all times. Writing a message word for action is the best way to make sure you do not mangle it.

Skill Tip: Being prepared:

The reality is that not everyone likes to leave a message on voice mail. Always be ready to take a message or information from a customer.

Skill 8: Controlling the Conversation

Rapport building is good, but it is your responsibility to build rapport while remaining in control of the call. If a caller gets off subject, take control of the conversation. If things get off track, ask a question related to the purpose of the call as a subtle buffer to get it back on track. Customers appreciate your handling their needs efficiently.

Skill Example:

(You) "When would you like us to deliver your new monitor?"

(Caller's Response) "Well, let's see, I have an uncle coming into town. He's a professional fishing guide, and his specialty is shark fishing. You ever go deep sea fishing?"

Skill Example A. Controlling the conversation (with a gentle, related question):

(Your Reply) "You know, I haven't, but that sounds very interesting, and it would be a great reason to set up everything early, wouldn't it? In fact, you might want to set up your monitor before your uncle comes in. So, do you want us to deliver that new monitor Wednesday afternoon or Friday morning?"

Skill 9: Avoiding Mouth Noises

Mouth noises annoy and alienate the other person. The mouthpiece of a telephone is a microphone that amplifies sounds on the receiving end. While on a call, do not eat, drink, hum or chew gum.

Skill Tip: Work to avoid annoying mouth noises.

Skill 10: Leaving a Positive Last Impression

A positive last impression counts as much as a good first impression. End your conversation on a positive note. Let the caller feel that you are glad and that you look forward to hearing from them again. This last impression is often the way they remember the entire call.

Skill Tip:

(You) "I'll let our crew member know, and he'll take care of it for you. He's very good. We appreciate your business, Ms Clinton. Thanks for calling."

(Caller's Response) "Thank you!" (Your Reply) "You're welcome."
Essential Telephone Skills-

Telephone calls may be broken into three major parts-

1. The introduction, in which both parties establish their identity and the convenience of the call.
2. The purpose, which involves communicating needs by asking well-constructed questions.
3. The conclusion, whereby both parties reach a verbal agreement on the points made during the call and any specific action that needs to be taken.

<u>**Here we discuss some essential telephone skills:**</u>

Making a Telephone call

Before making a telephone call, consider its purpose calls could possibly be made to obtain information, return a call, schedule an appointment, or service a customer. Be ready psychologically to make the call. Have a positive attitude toward making the call. Keep all the necessary information available when you make the call.

When making a call, be sure to do the following:

- Identify yourself immediately to get the call off to a positive start.
- Tell the purpose of the call to the person you call. Be specific.
- Ask well stated appropriate questions to obtain the desired action.
- Close the call in a friendly tone with an understanding between both parties of the action(s) that need to be taken.

Incoming Telephone Calls

Be prepared to answer the telephone when it rings. Keep pens and message pads close by as well as telephone directories and other reference materials. Use an answering machine if necessary. When answering the phone, follow these guidelines:

- Answer the telephone no later than the second ring.
- Identify yourself in a friendly tone.
- Use the caller's name.
- Gather as much information as possible.
- Do not interrupt the caller.
- Give accurate information.

It is an excellent idea to write down any questions prior to beginning the call or during the call. During the call, when both parties are asking questions, it is equally important to listen attentively. Attentive listening can be demonstrated by speaking in such a way that the listener knows you are hearing.

Question Skills

Questions should be asked in such a way as to obtain the desired information. Normally there are three major types of questions:

- Open questions: These questions call for more than a yes/no answer and often begin with who, what, where, when, why or how.

- Closed questions: These questions are used primarily to verify the information. Often these questions begin with are you, do you, can, could, did, will, or would.
- Forced-choice questions: These questions call for an either-or response. The listener has the choice between at least two options.

Maintaining Telephone Numbers

Telephone numbers may be obtained from your own record, from directories, or from directory assistance. Have the telephone number visible when you get ready to make the call. Developing a personal telephone list is very helpful. Telephone directories that contain both white pages and yellow pages can also be sources of excellent information. Use the white pages to locate a specific name of a person. Use the yellow pages to locate a product or service. Directory assistance provides access to a telephone number by going through a directory assistance operator. Usually, there is a fee for obtaining this information.

Operator Assisted Calls

Operator-assisted calls are the most expensive type of telephone calls. Avoid them if possible. Types of operator-assisted calls include the following:

- Collect calls: In collect calls, the person called must agree to accept the charges for the call.
- Third-number billing: Such a call is billed to a third party.
- Person-to-person: Such a call involves telling the operator you will speak only to a designated person. If that person is unavailable, you will not have to pay for the call.

Screening Calls

Screening a call means using judgment to determine whether you should put the caller through to the desired person by being friendly to the caller without revealing embarrassing or unnecessary information.

Transferring Calls

Transferring a call means that, for any number of reasons, it would be best for the caller to speak with someone else. It is important to be thoroughly familiar with the specific procedure for transferring a call.

Message Taking

Messages may either be left as voice-mail messages for the person being called or written down by someone else. If you are writing down the message, use a telephone message form to fill in the appropriate parts.

Specialized Telephone Calls

Handling the wide variety of both incoming and outgoing specialized telephone calls requires in-depth skill. The following are some of the more common types of specialized calls:

- Information calls: Calls made to gather information require careful thought to determine exactly what information you are trying to obtain.
- Scheduling appointment calls: Know exactly when you want an appointment before placing the call. Have all information in front of you when you place the call. If you are making calls for another individual, notify that person of the scheduled appointment. Likewise, be certain you have carefully recorded on an appointment calendar the designated scheduled time as well as any special instructions.
- Complaint calls: Often, a complaint call can become a negative experience by nature. Be prepared to deal with emotions in as positive a fashion as possible.
- Collection calls: Collecting money over the telephone is a challenging experience. Good questioning skills are of paramount importance in handling a collection call.
- Telemarketing calls: Selling a product or service over the telephone is done by a skilled salesperson called a telemarketer. Generally, telemarketers have been trained to deal with a wide variety of responses and situations.

It is wise to follow these steps when dealing with specialized calls:

- Always respond in a courteous and professional manner.
- Give accurate information.
- Be prepared to deal with rejection and negative responses.
- Offer a variety of positive solutions.

- End all calls courteously.

<u>Telephone Skills and the Future</u>

Telephone skills will undoubtedly continue to be increasingly important as technology and equipment continue to evolve. Strong communication skills will always be highly essential when using the telephone. Evolving technology will enhance the telephone in the future. Telephone skills must be integrated with that technology to make the process work.

PHONE ETIQUETTE

Telephone etiquette means being respectful to the person you are talking with, showing consideration for the other person's interest, allowing that person time to speak, communicating clearly and much, much more. Your voice must create a pleasant visual impression over the telephone.

Good phone etiquette is important because we cannot see the facial expressions and body language of the other person and vice versa. We must balance our voice by choosing our words carefully during conversation and using much more tone variation to convey our message. Here are some tried and tested tips on telephone etiquette to help us become aware of the courtesies that could easily be overlooked.

- Check the number carefully & then dial it correctly
- Allow it to ring long enough to give the called person time to get to the phone
- Do not ask them to wait the moment they answer
- Identify yourself immediately. Do not make them guess who is calling
- Ask if it is convenient to talk now.
- Talk loud enough directly into the phone to be heard without shouting
- If you have dialled a wrong number. Apologize. Do not just hang up.

Always remember you are talking to a person now, not a machine. So, speak accordingly Observe courtesies like "Hello, Please, Thank you, and Good bye"

Etiquettes while making a Call:

- Be an attentive listener; do not do other jobs at the same time

- Do not interrupt while the other person is speaking. Use common courtesy.
- Use the caller's name.
- If they have to be put on hold, ask if you can call them back rather than keep them waiting indefinitely on the line.
- If they would like to wait on the line, get back to them every 30 seconds to update them and give them another opportunity to be called back.
- Bad news should be delivered face-to-face if possible and not over the telephone.

Etiquettes while receiving a call:

- Answer your phone promptly to save the time of both the caller and yourself.
- Greet the caller pleasantly.
- If you have company, let the caller know that you must be brief or that you will call back later.
- Take messages for others clearly and politely.
- Be sure to pass on the message.
- Always return telephone calls and do so as soon as possible.
- If it is necessary to transfer the call, first tell the caller that you are transferring the call and then do it.
- Let the caller be the one to end the call first.
- Remember to farewell the caller with, "Goodbye" or something similar.
- Hang up the phone gently.

E-MAIL SKILLS

An e-mail is a digital message sent electronically from one computer to one or more other computers. E-mails are flexible and can be used for giving instructions, serving as documentation, providing confirmation, communicating rules and procedures, making recommendations, providing a status update, making an inquiry. Like a memorandum, it is more precise than an oral conversation, it provides a record of the communication, and it can send a single message to a large number of people. During the 1960s, Ray Tomlinson invented e-mail. E-mail operates across computer networks, which today is primarily the Internet. There are primarily three types of e-mails:

a. Direct e-mails: These are the personal e-mails that are sent from one person to another, with content that is designed to do a specific thing, like thank for a meeting, book lunch, introduce the organization, or convey an attachment. They are customized, specific to the sender and recipient, and sent directly from a person's e-mail address.

b. Broadcast e-mails: These are the newsletters, alerts, advertisements, and other materials that are floated to many different persons or organization. The key point behind this type of e-mail is the one-to-many nature of it.

c. Sequence e-mails: Sometimes called nurture e-mails or drip marketing e-mails, these are a series of e-mails that are sent to a specific person. For example, if your organization does a repeated event – say a seminar for prospective clients – then the attendees likely have an interest.

The main features of e-mail are:

i. Attachment: Ability to attach the files along the messages.
ii. Address book: It is also the most important features of e-mail that allows a user to store the information along with the e-mail addresses.

Basic E-Mail Skills-

Let us discuss how e-mail works and what basic skills we need for using e-mail.

To send or receive an e-mail, we must have an account on a mail server. This is similar to our mailing address where we receive letters. Our e-mail message is sent from our computer to a server where the computer looks at the e-mail address and then directs the message on to the server associated with the recipient's e-mail account. Once our e-mail arrives at its destination mail server, the message is stored in an electronic mailbox until the recipient retrieves it. We can still receive e-mail while our computer is turned off. The mail server collects and stores our incoming e-mail until the next time we access your e-mail by opening our mailbox and downloading our messages.

We can send an e-mail to anyone in the world, as long as we have his or her e-mail address.

1. Understanding E-mail Addresses

An e-mail address has two main components:

- The user name comes before the "@" sign. When we sign up for an e-mail account, we are usually asked to supply a user name (our first initial and last name is often used). The domain name comes after the "@" sign. This refers to the mail server, the computer that stores our electronic mailbox. It is usually the name of a company or organization.
- Finally, there is a dot (.) followed by letters that indicate the type of domain (.com, .edu, .net, .org, .lib, .in, .us, and so on). Example of an e-mail address: abc@gmail.com or abc.123@yahoo.com etc.

2. Composing and Sending an E-mail Message

Followings are the basic steps for composing an e-mail:

- To create a new e-mail, click the red "Compose Mail" button (on the left-hand side of the screen). Type the recipient's e-mail address in the "To:" box.
- To send a message to more than one person, you may enter multiple addresses by placing a comma and space between each address. (E.g,: To: jdoe@example.com, me@example.com, dd@example.com)
- Ensure that you correctly enter the e-mail address or the message will be sent either to a different person or returned back to you with a note that it was undeliverable.
- Type the subject of the message in the "Subject:" box. Keeps the subject to a word or phrase summarizing the content of your message (E.g.: Subject: Today's Work Progress).

- Use your mouse and click inside the message box it is where you will write your e-mail letter, i.e. the body of the message.
- When you are finished typing your message and are ready to send it, click the red "Send" button.

3. Reading an E-mail Message

To read an e-mail, click on the subject of the e-mail. [Note: Unread messages in your Inbox will be highlighted.]

4. Replying to a Message

- Open the message that you want to reply.
- Click the "Reply" button, which looks like an arrow pointing to the left. The program will present you with a message already addressed to the sender. The subject line will state "Re:" and then the old message's subject. You will probably not change the subject line, so the receiver knows that you are replying to a previously an e-mail that was previously sent.
- [Note: the difference between "Reply" and "Reply All." Clicking the "Reply" button will send your reply only to the original sender of the message. Clicking the "Reply All" button will send your reply to everyone who received the original message.]
- Click in the box above the text to which you are replying.
- Complete you reply message.
- Click "Send" when you are finished typing your message and are ready to send it.

5. Forwarding a Message

- Open the message you wish to forward to another person.
- Click the down arrow next to the reply arrow.
- Click on "Forward".

- Type the recipient's address or addresses (if there is more than one recipient) in the "To:" box.
- Type a note above the forwarded message (optional).
- Click "Send".

On the Internet, everything moves at the speed of light, including e-mail. Because e-mail can be sent and received so quickly, it is often written in a more conversational manner than a formal letter. An e-mail with grammatical errors can be viewed as being "sloppy" and so you should ensure that your e-mail is written in a manner that will be deemed appropriate by the person that reads it. Always double check your e-mail before clicking the send button. Use proper grammar; capitalize the letters as and when it is required.

Advanced E-Mail Skill-

Now we are familiar with e-mail basics. There are many advanced features available with e- mail. Let us discuss here these features.

Attachment

An e-mail attachment is a computer file sent along with an e-mail message. One or more files can be attached to any e-mail message and be sent along with it to the recipient. This is typically used as a simple method to share documents and images. We can send one or more files containing texts or images, such as a photograph, sent as part of an e-mail message. However, there are some limitations related to the size of the file. These files are quite common and safe:

- .txt - Plain text file.
- .jpg (or .jpeg) - Image file for photos etc.
- .gif - graphic file.

Click the "Open" or "Choose File" or another similar button to attach the file to your e-mail. Then, continue composing your e-mail (put the e-mail address of the person you want to send the attachment to in the To: field, add a subject and message in the body, and hit Send).

Sending a copy of the mail-

We can send the same contents of the mail to others in two different methods: Cc and Bcc: Cc means CARBON COPY and Bcc means BLIND CARBON COPY. We can use Cc when we want to copy the mail to others publicly, means all the recipients will know, who others are also getting the same mail.

When we use Bcc, it means we want to mail it privately. Any recipients on the Bcc line of an e-mail are not visible to others on the e-mail. For security and privacy reasons, it is best to use the Blind Carbon Copy (Bcc) feature when sending an e-mail message to a large number of people. When we place e-mail addresses in the Bcc field of a message, those addresses are invisible to the recipients of the e-mail.

Essential E-Mail Skills and Tips-

Here are some tips for Effective E-mail Communication:

Write a clear and concise message.

The message you want to mail should be clear and concise. This saves your time as well as the receivers. You can write this by the following skills: Use bulleted points to clearly express your thoughts and outline the points you are trying to get across in an easy to understand format.

Always reread your message and double-check for grammar and misused words before sending an e-mail.

Use spell check after composing your message. You should also make it standard procedure to reread your entire message before sending. This practice reduces the chance of making mistakes.

Copy back salient points when replying to an earlier message.

It is frustrating when someone sends you an e-mail, with a specific answer but you are unable to recall the original issue. This problem can be avoided by copying a portion of the original message alluding to the context.

Use specific subject line descriptions.

Since many e-mail messages go back and forth several times over the course of many weeks, it is important to describe what the reader will find inside the mail accurately.

Ensure the recipient or recipients before sending mail.

E-mail is also ridiculously easy to edit and forward. Keep in mind that sending a message to one person can eventually be viewed by many other unintended parties. Always double-check the recipient line before sending any e-mail.

Never send mail when you are upset.

It is never a good idea to send an e-mail when you are angry or upset. Only later, after we calm down, we revisit the message and realize that we dramatically overreacted. But it would be too late to do anything now, except apologize and try to mend. This is more common than you think.

If you compose an e-mail in anger, wait a predetermined period of time before sending it.

<u>Avoid shortcuts and abbreviations e-mail messages.</u>

Sometimes shortcuts and abbreviations can be used to write or forward a message to our friends for personal e-mail. However, such shortcuts and abbreviations are never to be used to business or official communications. Some common shortcuts like "LOL, BRB, OMG, 2, 4, SMH and u r" are used in personal communication but are simply too casual for most business communication.

<u>Never forward Viral Messages.</u>

Nowadays, many fake messages float in social media. It's not wise to forward such messages to your contacts. Unless and until you are sure about the messages you received then only forward those messages if it is required.

E-MAIL ETIQUETTE:

E-mail etiquette refers to the principles of behaviour that one should use when writing or answering e-mail messages. It is also known as the code of conduct for e-mail communication. E-mail etiquette depends upon to whom we are writing mail, i.e. friends & relatives, partners, customers, superior, or subordinates.

We must follow e-mail etiquette in our professional communication because it is a form of communication which is a reflection of senders and responders. Bad e-mail etiquette reflects badly on us, and a record of this is kept in mailboxes over which we have no control. Good e- mail etiquette reflects well on us, improves our public perception and persona and increases the chance of a prompt and comprehensive response. It is not hard to maintain good e-mail etiquette once we know what it is. A company needs to implement etiquette rules for the following three reasons:

- Professionalism: By using proper e-mail language, your company will convey a professional image.
- Efficiency: E-mails that are to the point are much more effective than poorly worded e- mails.
- Protection from liability: Employee's awareness of e-mail risks will protect your company from costly lawsuits.

Before Composing E-Mail:

One thing before you start means before composing or responding to an e-mail, ask yourself this: is e-mail the right medium for this communication? If you are not sure, pick up the phone or walk over to the person and have a conversation. E-mail only if it is the right medium.

The first step in writing an e-mail message:

Identify the purpose of the message in the e-mail you are going to send. In other words, focus your objective, i.e. try to follow the five I's: Inform Inquire, Influence, Instruct, and Incite.

Focus your content. Do not let unnecessary ideas impose on your principal message.

To:

Each individual on the To box of an e-mail is responsible for the response or taking an action (or part of an action) outlined on the Subject line and the message relates directly to them.

CC:

Cc means Carbon copy and the same message will be received by the recipients along with the recipients mentioned in the To box of the mail. No action or response is expected of individuals on the CC the recipient needs only to read or file the message. The individuals whose work is indirectly affected by the communication should be included on the CC.

BCC:

BCC means Blind Carbon Copy and the same message will be delivered to the recipients mentioned in the Bcc, CC and To box of the e-mail. However, the recipients are invisible to the other recipients mentioned in the BCC. So always use Bcc field cautiously.

Subject:

A subject line effectively summarizes the message. If the subject line is clearly written, each recipient will have a clear understanding of the objective that the message relates to.

- Subject line should effectively summarize the message
- Do not use more than six or seven words in a subject line
- Never use capital letter
- When replying, change the subject line when the topic changes.

Salutations:

We should be very careful in writing the salutation (greeting) because it can be mistranslated by the reader. So, the sender must ensure that his/her reader is comfortable and happy with the salutation, otherwise, rest of the communication may not bring any positive result.

<u>Privacy:</u>

E-mail is not and never has been private. Once you send an e-mail, the recipient can and will do what they want with it. If you need to share private information, pick up the phone, use a different secure system, or use coded attachments.

Use your corporate e-mail for work only. Never use it for personal stuff. Corporate e-mail is not private, it is archived, it is monitored, and most have policies against it. Use your private

e-mail for personal affairs; never send personal messages to a recipient's corporate addresses. Use the blind copy (BCC) or mail merge function to protect the privacy of your contacts.

<u>Attachments:</u>

When you are sending an attachment, tell the recipient what the name of the file is? What program it is saved in, and the version of the program. Compress large attachments and send attachments only when they are necessary. Use a good virus scanner as mails with viruses are not appreciable, and the receiver may become annoyed.

<u>Reply or Reply to all:</u>

Ask yourself: "Does everyone need to know this information?"

- Each e-mail should be replied to within at least 24 hours and preferably within the same working day.
- If the e-mail is complicated, send an e-mail saying that you have received it and that you will get back to them. This will put the people's mind at rest, and usually, they will be patient.
- Respond only to messages that require one. When replying, make sure that you are adding value to the conversation, truly moving it forward.
- While replying to an e-mail message with an attachment, which is to accompany your reply, you must forward the message instead of using the "Reply" or "Reply All" button. Otherwise, the attachment is not included with the message.
- Do not reply to spam.

The Closing:

In the business world, ending an e-mail professionally is just as important as perfecting the rest of the message. If you do it sloppily, you might lose some precious business opportunities. Courtesy is always important, no matter how short the e-mail is. Before you end your e-mail, you can add some sentence as follows: Thank you for your patience and cooperation, Thank you for your consideration. Include an accurate follow-up statement:

- I will send you additional information.
- I look forward to receiving your input.
- If you have questions or concerns, do let me know.
- I look forward to hearing from you.
- Please let me know if you need further assistance on this.
- If a response is required, specify what, when.

Do not forget to attach documents:

If you plan to attach a document, attach it as soon as you refer to the document in the e-mail. So, often people forget to attach even when they indicate an attachment.

Signatures:

A professional signature makes it easy to contact you. Your e-mail account can automatically add these data to the bottom of the e-mail: Full professional name, Job title, Business phone/fax numbers, Business street address, Business website (if any), A legal disclaimer (if required by your company).

POINTS TO REMEMBER:

- Phone and e-mail conversations are every bit as important as face-to-face interaction. The goal should always be to bolster relationships with customers and never to provide a bad customer experience. Every conversation will mould the public's perception of your company and build (or destroy) your brand.
- While e-mail and mail communication may be efficient, the telephone is still an ideal way to contact customers. Phone calls create stronger relationships, foster clear communication, and allow you and your customers to save time by getting the answers you need in real-time.

- The invention of the telephone provided an important device for facilitating human communication. No longer did people need to be co-located beside each other to be able to converse. Through the use of the telephone, people could have equally meaningful conversations at a distance, all the while preserving reciprocity.
- One of the most important contributions the telephone has brought to the lives of people is the ability to call during emergencies. Telephones are very helpful during emergency situations because they are able to connect to the department you are calling than going to the place with yourself.
- How has the telephone changed and improved our lives? The telephone changed society for the better by making it easier for people to communicate. The telephone made it possible for two people to communicate directly, making it easier to interpret messages based on the speaker's tone of voice and overall demeanour.
- There are pros and cons for both e-mail and telephone communication. The most important thing is context - why you need to communicate, and what you are communicating. Some things are best discussed through e-mail, and some are best left for the phone.

<u>GLOSSARY:</u>

- **Telephone**- These are devices used to communicate messages across lines electronically. Alexander Graham Bell invented the first telephone in 1876 in Boston.
- **Basic Telephone Skills**- This refers to communicate effectively on the telephone to customers by following some skills.
- **ARPANET**- A research organization Advanced Research Projects Agency Network
- **Videsh Sanchar Nigam Limited (VSNL)**- India's telephone organization started internet for the public in 1971.
- **Buffer words**- These refer to three parts of greeting: "Good Morning", "Good Afternoon" or "Good Evening".
- **Advanced Telephone Skills**- This refers to develop the core skills to influence on the telephone and further build rapport with clients or customers.
- **Feedback Signals**- This refers to the response to the caller during a telephone conversation.

- **Essential Telephone Skills**- This refers to the most professional skills while making conversation over telephone with the customers.
- **Telephone Etiquette**- This refers to the respect to be shown to the caller during a telephone conversation. This includes the way we speak to the customer to make a good rapport.
- **E-mail**- This is the new and advanced method of communication in a digital mode, and messages are sent electronically from one computer to one or more other computers.
- **Direct e-mails**- This refers to one-to-one communication includes mainly personal messages.
- **Broadcast e-mails**- This refers to one-to-many communication, includes mainly advertisement, newsletters, etc.
- **Sequence e-mails**- This refers to the communication to selective persons from any organization, etc.
- **Mail Server**- This refers to a remote or central computer that holds electronic mail (e- mail) messages for clients on a network is called a mail server. A mail server is similar to the post office, where mail is stored and sorted before being sent to its final destination.
- **E-mail Address**- This is a unique identifier for an e-mail account. It is used to both send and receive e-mail messages over the Internet. In other words, we can say this refers to a name that identifies an electronic post office box on a network where e-mail can be sent.

- **Domain name**- This refers to the website name. A domain name is the address where Internet users can access the website. This is also used for finding and identifying computers on the Internet.
- **Mail attachment**- This refers to a computer file sent along with an e-mail message. One or more files can be attached to any e-mail message and be sent along with it to the recipient. This is typically used as a simple method to share documents and images.
- **Cc and Bcc**- Cc means Carbon Copy and Bcc means Blind Carbon Copy. Cc and Bcc are almost similar except that the e-mail address of the recipients specified in the Bcc field does not appear in the received message header and the recipients in the To or Cc fields will not know that a copy sent to these addresses.

INTERVIEW SKILLS

INTRODUCTION

Interview is a kind of assessment to assess a candidate's personality, skills, attitude, overall conduct, interests and to determine whether he/she is fit for the job? It is a kind of conversation that occurs between a prospective employee (candidate) and an employer or organization. There are several mediums to assess a candidate- one of them is interview. Interviews are also various kinds, such as- Telephone Interview, Face-to-Face Interview, Panel Interview, Lunch/Dinner Interview, Informal Interview, Portfolio Based Interview, etc.

OBJECTIVES:

After successful completion of this chapter, you will be able to-

- Prepare yourself for the interview.
- Know about various interview skills.
- Know about interview essentials.

INTERVIEW PREPARATION:

There are the following tips to prepare well for the interview-
    Carefully analyse the job description
    You should go through the job description, where the employer describes the qualifications and desirables.
    Make a match with the job

After going through the job description, prepare a list of your assets and match them to the job requirements.

Prepare examples of your accomplishments

Better to saying something, share your accomplishment that proves your skills. Focus on how you utilized your skills in such a harsh situation; get success as a leader/team member.

Research the Company

Use any search engine (e.g. Google, DuckDuckGo, Bing, and YouTube) to gather relevant information about the organization, look for product or service reviews, collect information about the organization and their competitors, read their annual reports/ progress reports (if available).

Examine the organization's website

In today's scenario, almost all organizations have their own website. Start with the home page of the website and carefully read the "About us", "Vision", "Mission" page, etc. Also, get familiar with the products or services, press release (if any) and key officers/founders.

Check the LinkedIn and Facebook Company Profiles

After getting the information about the company from various sources, you will be able to understand more and more things about the company. Company's social media accounts help a lot to understand about services/ products offered by the company.

Use Google, YouTube, and LinkedIn and other social media platforms to research any names (if you have)

Hopefully, you know the names of the people who will be interviewing you. You may find that you have something in common with someone interviewing you. Try to get a sense of the kind of people who work there. Also, try (If interviewer has written and posted) to read the articles on LinkedIn or any other websites written by the interviewer.

Practice Interviewing

Do practice answering interview questions that you probably think may be asked. This activity will enhance your confidence level during the interview.

Get your interview clothes ready

Have an interview outfit ready to wear at all times, so you don't have to think about what you are going to wear while you are scrambling to get ready for a job interview.

Decide what to bring for a job interview

Make a list of things you need to bring for an interview before getting ready for the interview so, that you can get relaxed at the time of job interview.

Practice interview etiquette

Remember to greet your interviewer and everyone else you meet politely, pleasantly and enthusiastically. Proper interview etiquettes are important. During the interview, watch your body language; shake hands firmly and make eye contact as you articulate your points. pay attention, be attentive, and look interested.

Listen and Ask Questions

Listening is just as important as answering questions during interview. If you are unable to pay attention, so, you are not going to be able to give a good response. Also, be ready to engage the interviewer, if one to one conversation is there.

Prepare for the salary expectation question and negotiation

Get ready to face the salary negotiation related questions. Prepare yourself well with the lower limit of the offered salary and what you expect. Also, get ready to justify your expected salary with acceptable justifications.

INTERVIEWING ESSENTIALS:

- **The handshake**- A strong, but not too strong handshake is a power move. Take control and give a firm handshake when you meet a manager and when you leave the interview.
- **Body language**- Simply sitting up straight, looking at who is speaking to you and keeping still makes a huge difference in your appearance.
- **Posture is important**- Sitting up straight and planting your feet gives you confidence without you even knowing it.
- **Be confident**- Never underestimate how valuable you are. Be confident in your work, personality, and skills.
- **Stay Positive**- Negative comments about former employers and lack of enthusiasm is not a good signal in the context of job interviews. Remain enthusiastic and maintain eye contact with interviewers as much as possible.
- **Always listen**- Always listen carefully, then start answering.

- **Stay Calm**- Even if the interviewers asked unexpected questions or role-play activities unannounced, present calm and collected appearance throughout the interview to prove your capability.
- **Carry a notebook, your resume, and a pen**- Always keep a notebook, CV (minimum 2 copies) and a pen with you.
- **Attitude**- Attitude is a very important factor during interview, show a positive attitude, smile and act happily.
- **Give specific examples** - Your answers should relate to your work so be specific and knowledgeable about what you have done.
- **Decide when to talk**, when to remain silent.
- **Answering the interview questions**- Some questions may take time for you to answer properly, do not be afraid to ask for a moment to ensure you have an accurate answer.
- **Presentation Skills**- Many interviews will involve giving some form of presentation – whether it's prepared or not. Ensuring you appear confident, eloquent, and informed is essential to scoring top marks during any presentations.
- **Follow up with a Thank You Note**- Send thank you note immediately after the interview. A thank you note can be sent via email.

TYPES OF INTERVIEWS:

a. **The Telephone Interview**- In today's scenario, telephone interviews are a popular one, because they speed up the interview process and minimise time-wastage. Telephonic interviews are quicker, cheaper, less effort for interviewer and the candidate, reach till long distance, etc.

b. **The Face-to-Face Interview**- These types of interviews are, by far the most popular and efficient form of assessment. Allowing you to get up close and personal with each candidate while keeping an eye on their body language is far more effective than any other interviewing format. You have enough time to build a relationship with interviewer so that you can answers confidently.

c. **The Panel Interview**- Panel interviews are the same as the individual, face-to-face interviews, but with two or more interviewers in the room. The main advantage of panel interviewing is that it precludes any personal biases that might creep into the assessment process. Each interviewer will pick up on different characteristics, strengths and weaknesses and together (hopefully) make a much fairer judgement.

d. **The Group Interview-** Several candidates, are present at this type of interview. You will be asked to interact with each other by usually a group discussion. You might even be given a task to do as a team, so make sure you speak up and give your opinion.

e. **The Sequential Interview-** These are several interviews in turn with a different interviewer each time. Usually, each interviewer asks questions to test different sets of competencies.

f. **Competency-Based Interviews-** Interviews that require you to give examples of specific skills are called competency-based interviews, or job-specific interviews or skill-based interviews. The interviewer will ask questions that will help them determine if you have the knowledge and skills required for the specific job or not.

g. **Formal / Informal Interviews-** Hiring managers (when the candidates have proven skills and a renowned name in the field) may begin the screening process with a relaxed, informal conversation instead of a formal interview. This is more of a casual discussion than a typical job interview. On a similar note, a chat over a cup of coffee is another less formal type of job interview.

h. **Portfolio Based Interviews-** In the digital or communications industry, it is likely that you will be asked to take your portfolio along or show it online. Make sure all your work is up to date without too little or too much. Make sure that your images if in print are big enough for the interviewer to see properly, and always test your online portfolio on all Internet browsers before turning up.

TIPS FOR GOOD JOB INTERVIEWS:

- Do your homework.
- Determine your value.
- Be prepared for tough questions and practice.
- Avoid bad habits.
- Be on time.
- Dress comfortably.
- Anticipate questions and prepare talking points.

- Rehearse with mock job interviews.
- Build your confidence.
- Make a strong first impression.

COMMON JOB INTERVIEW QUESTIONS:

1. What are your key experiences and accomplishments?
2. How did you hear about the vacancy?
3. Explain your reason for leaving your current job.
4. Why are you qualified for this position?
5. Tell me about the last time a co-worker or customer got angry with you. What happened?
6. Describe your dream job.
7. Where do you see yourself in five years?
8. Share your experience regarding the said position.
9. Out of all the other candidates, why should we hire you?
10. Why do you want to leave your current job?
11. What kind of work environment do you like best?
12. Tell me how you think other people would describe you.
13. What can we expect from you in your first three months?
14. What was your salary in your last job?
15. What are your salary requirements?
16. Why was there a gap in your employment?
17. How do you deal with pressure or stressful situations?
18. Tell me about a time you demonstrated leadership skills.
19. Have you any questions for me? (Yes/No; below questions can be asked by the candidate)
20. What do you expect me to accomplish in the first 90 days?
21. What really drives results in this job?
22. What are the company's highest-priority goals this year, and how would my role contribute?
23. What percentage of employees was brought in by current employees?
24. Please share with me the company's mission.

POINTS TO REMEMBER:

- Interview is a kind of assessment which assesses a candidate's personality, skills, attitude, overall conduct and interests in respect to the prospective job.
- Interviews are also various kinds, such as- Telephone Interview, Face-to-Face Interview, Panel Interview, Lunch/Dinner Interview, Informal Interview, Portfolio Based Interview, etc.
- There are some interview preparation skills, e.g. analyse the job description, research the company, examining the organization's website, practice interviewing, interview etiquette and more.
- Some of interview essentials are- body language, handshake manner, sitting posture, confidence level, positive attitude, etc.

<u>GLOSSARY:</u>

- **Portfolio Based Interviews**- Online collection of your documents, experience, and qualification in a well and presentable manner.
- **Competency Based Interviews**- Interviews that requires showing specific skills or competency.
- **Panel Interview**- Where two or more interviewers are taking interview at same time in the room.
- **Interview essentials**- Necessary things or tips to get ready for the interview.

The Author

Dr Anshumali Pandey, PhD, Author.

Dr. Anshumali Pandey, is a renowned & reliable name in the field of Education, Hospitality, Tourism and Tribal Food. He is a Teacher and Chef by profession, and also an Author, a Business Auditor, and an avid culinary traveller to the Indian Sub continental hinterlands. Dr. Anshumali Pandey is a Hospitality Educator (PhD) who specialises in Higher Education, Office Administration, Pay roll, HR, Labour Laws, Audit, and Procurement & Tender Process. He is an Author with 44 Publications consisting of 29 Books.

The books written by Dr Anshumali Pandey are essentially a banquet arising from an experience of over 25 years of Professional life and have boiled down to crisp and accurate writing on his favourite subjects. Hospitality Sector champion requires to be a specialist in many fields and Dr Pandey is one of them. His knowledge is evident from the spectrum of subjects which he has chosen for his books so far, which ranges from being a specialist chef, to Master of Human resources, to Education and to love for children, and topped with Spirituality.

Books written by the Author are –

1. Theory of Indian Cookery
2. Beauty and Irony of Silvassa Tourism
3. A Short Indian Food Story
4. Be Your Own Guide to Indian Cuisine
5. Cookery Fundamentals
6. History of Indian Food
7. The Great Indian Story Book for Children
8. Personal Budget: Easy Work Book
9. Online Classes Log Book
10. Dictionary Making Work Book for School Children
11. The Lazy Bed
12. Hindu Dharm (In Hindi Language)
13. Where is my coffee?
14. Your First Job is Never your Last (Volume 1)
15. You are Almost There (Quick Fix Resume and Interview Hacks)
16. Working for the Enemy? - A lesson in Career Management
17. Public Speaking for the Young
18. A Date With Coffee
19. How to be The Best Hotel Front Office Employee
20. Diploma in Food Production, The complete Syllabus
21. Diploma in F&B Service, The Complete Syllabus
22. Diploma in Front Office, The Complete Syllabus
23. The Time to Speak is Now
24. Munshi Premchand (Short Stories in English)
25. The Housekeeping Department, Text Book
26. Hitchhiker's Guide to Trekking in Uttarakhand
27. Uttarakhand, A divine Land for a Reason
28. Bachhon ke liye rochak kahaniyan (In Hindi Language)
29. Basic Communication Skills of English

Connect with me: anshumali.pandey@gmail.com
https://notionpress.com/author/337004

Scan the QR code to know more with updated information